I0468929

Introduction

Within the pages of this book you will find a variety of original vintage Art Nouveau designs of ladies from the late 19th Century for your own colouring creativity.

Simply relax, de-stress yourself and use your own imagination when colouring in these wonderful designs.

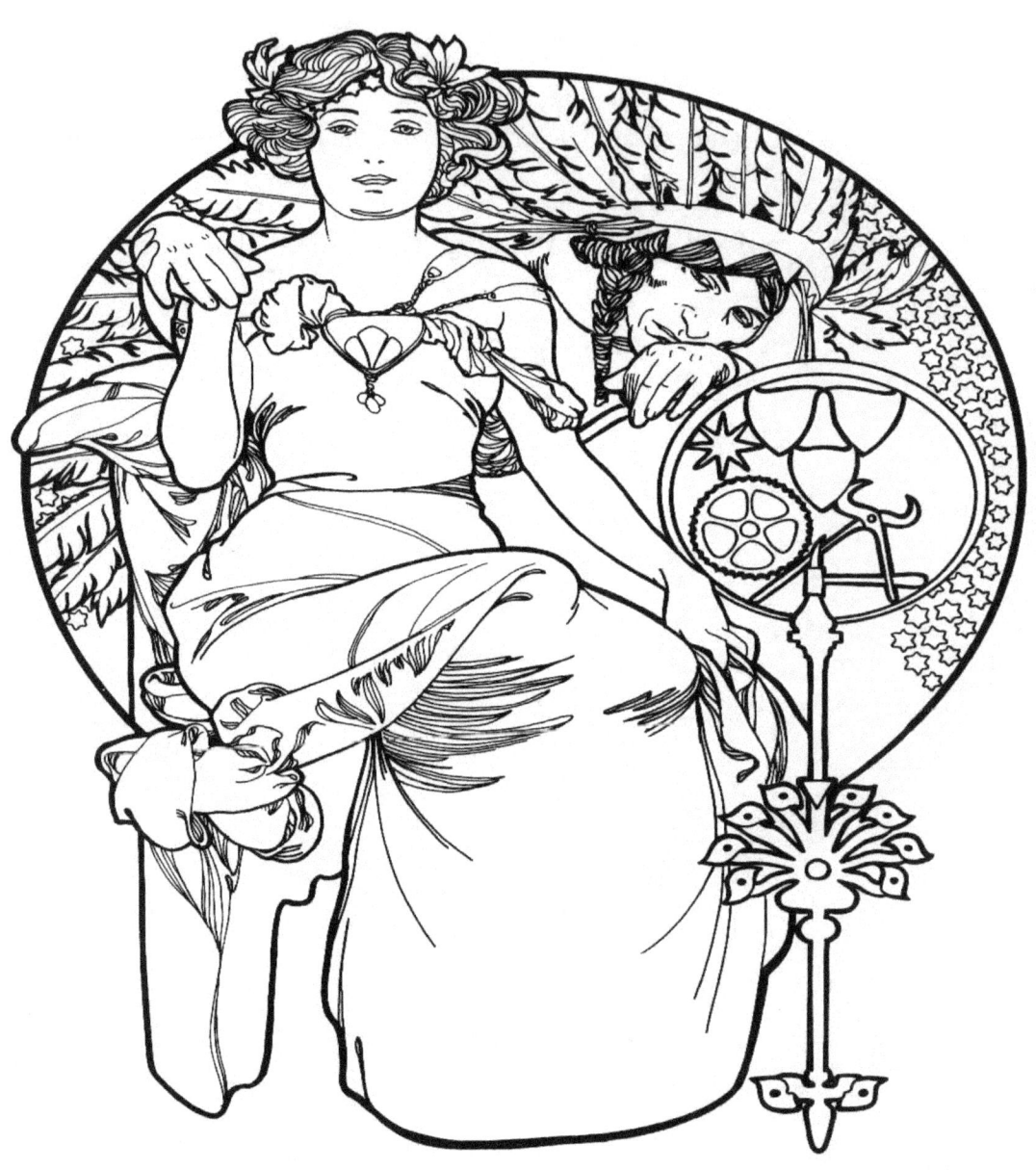

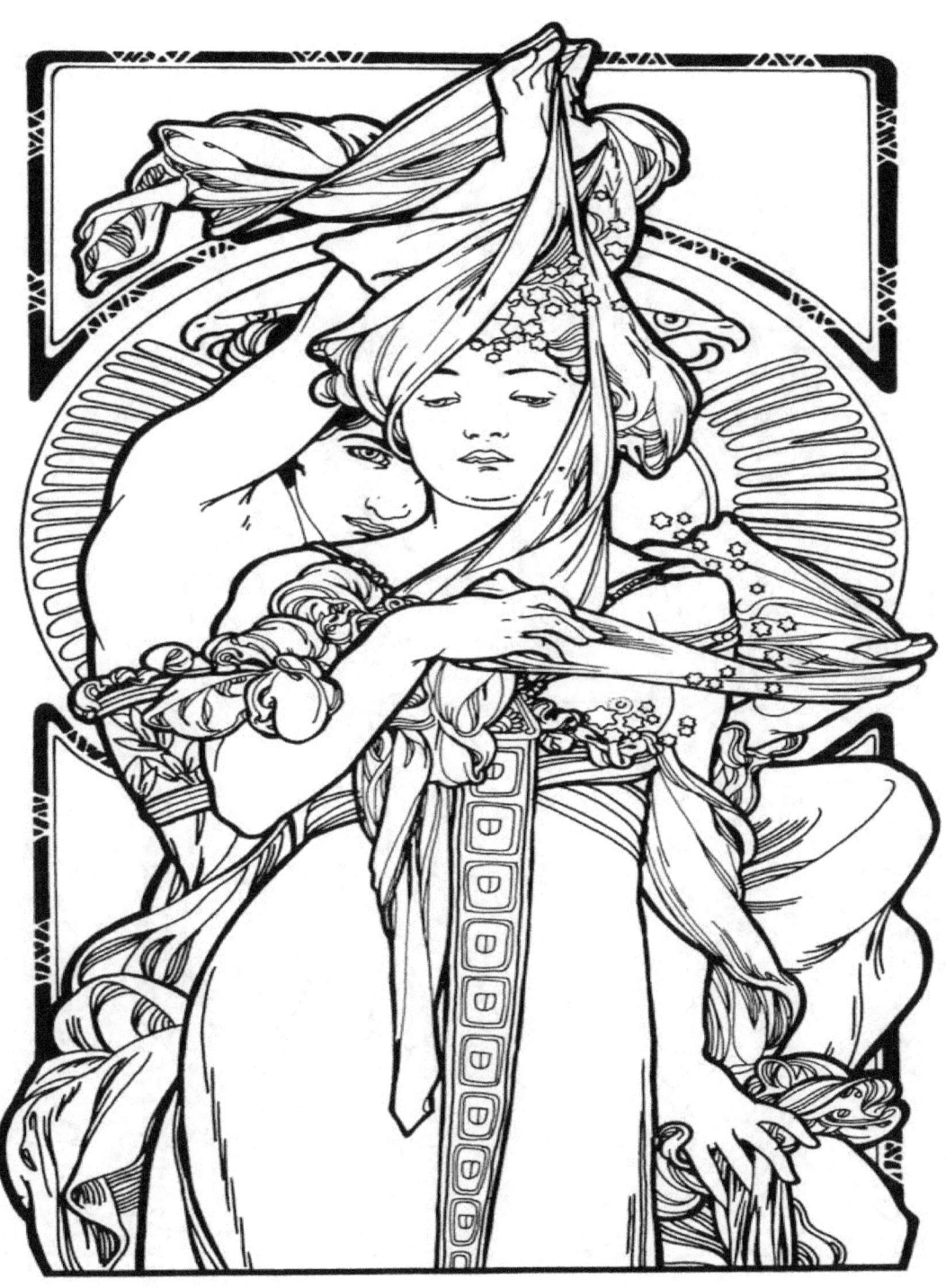

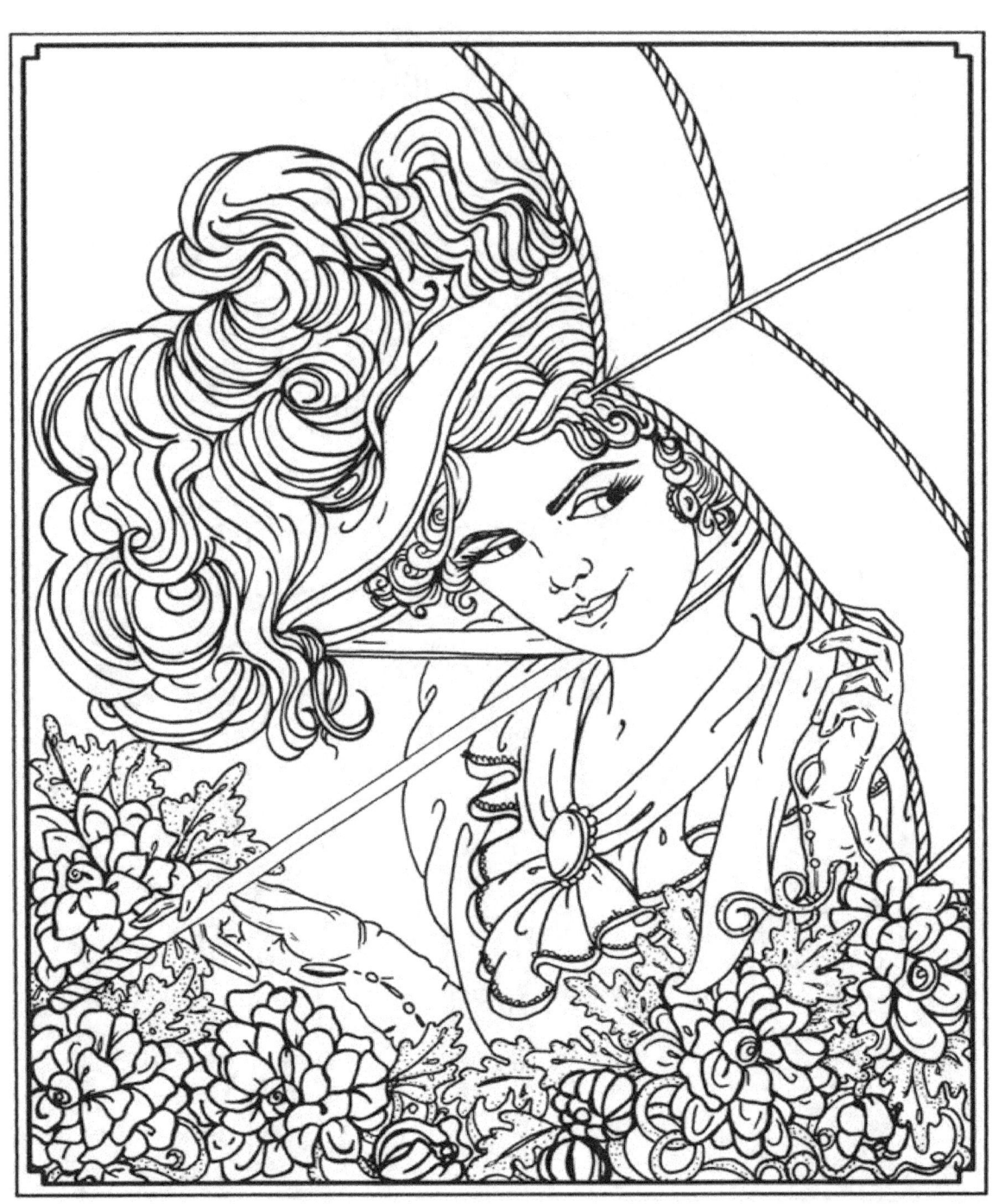

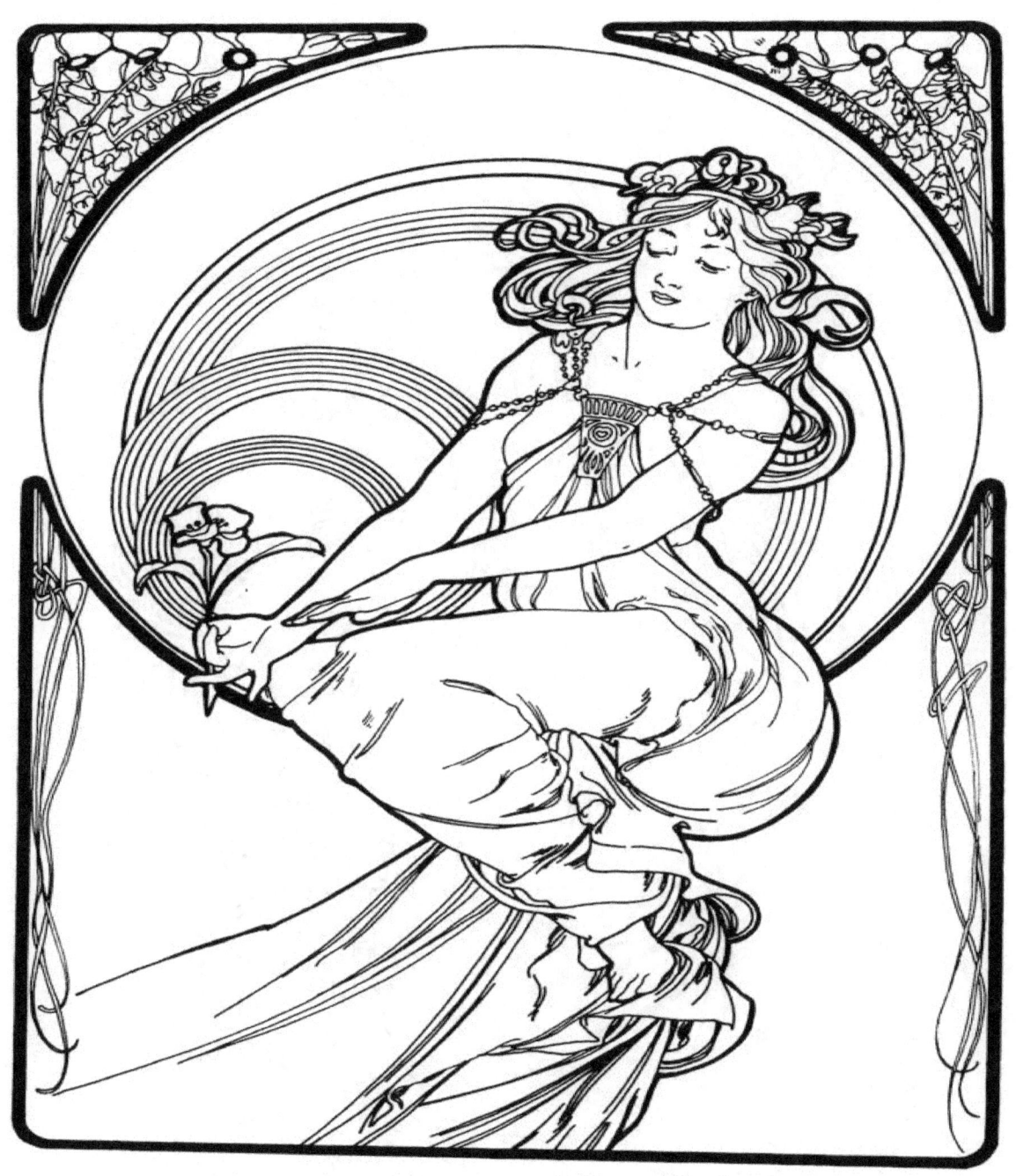

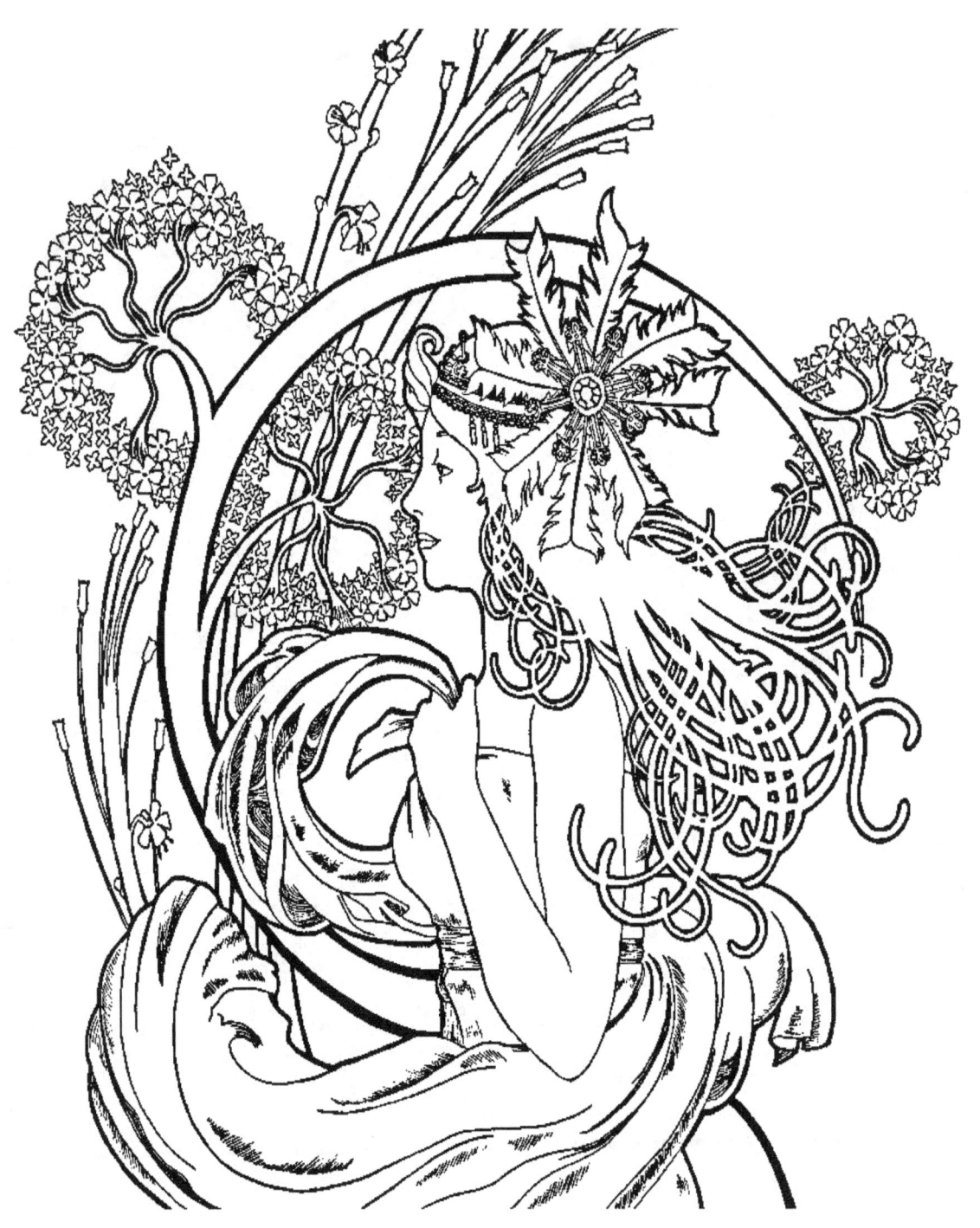

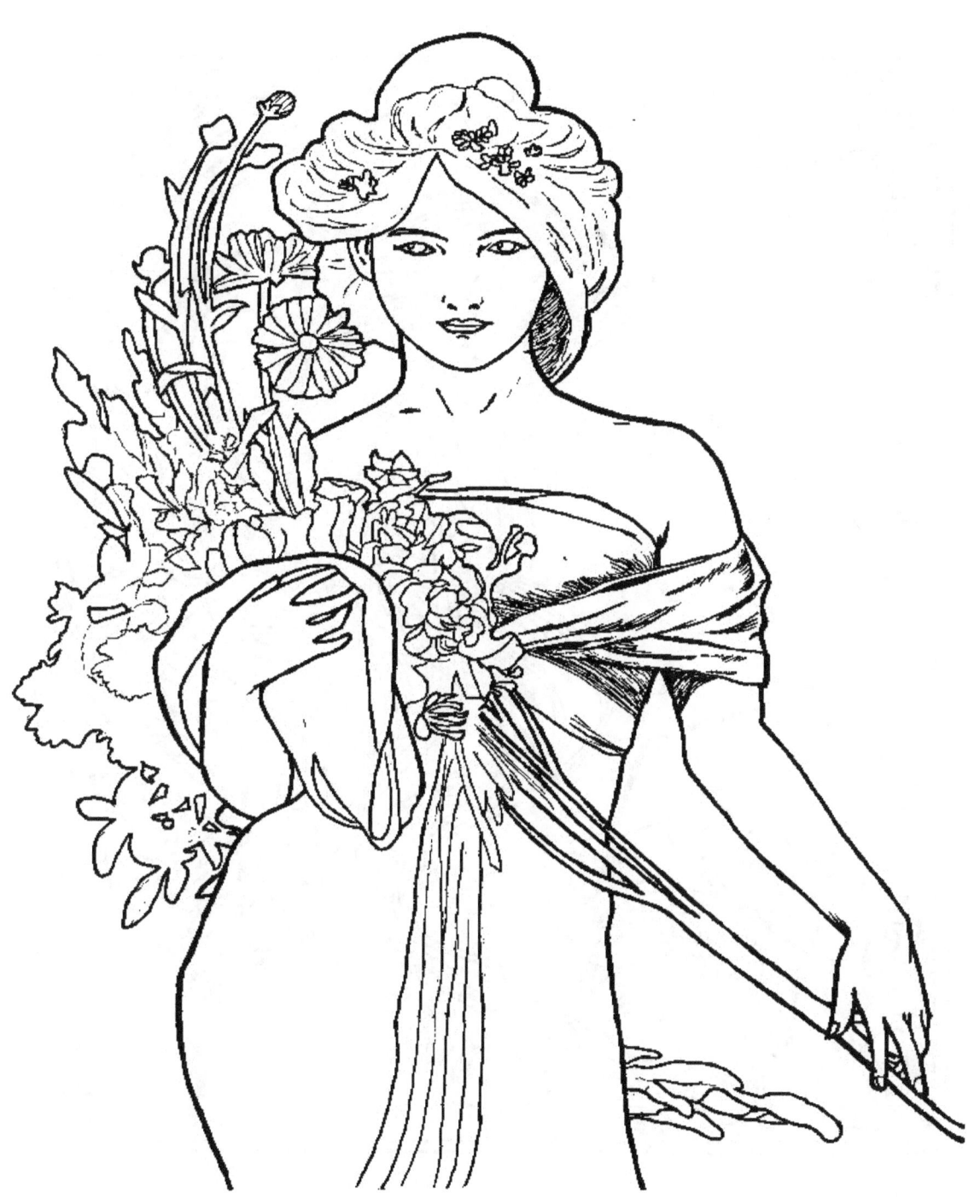

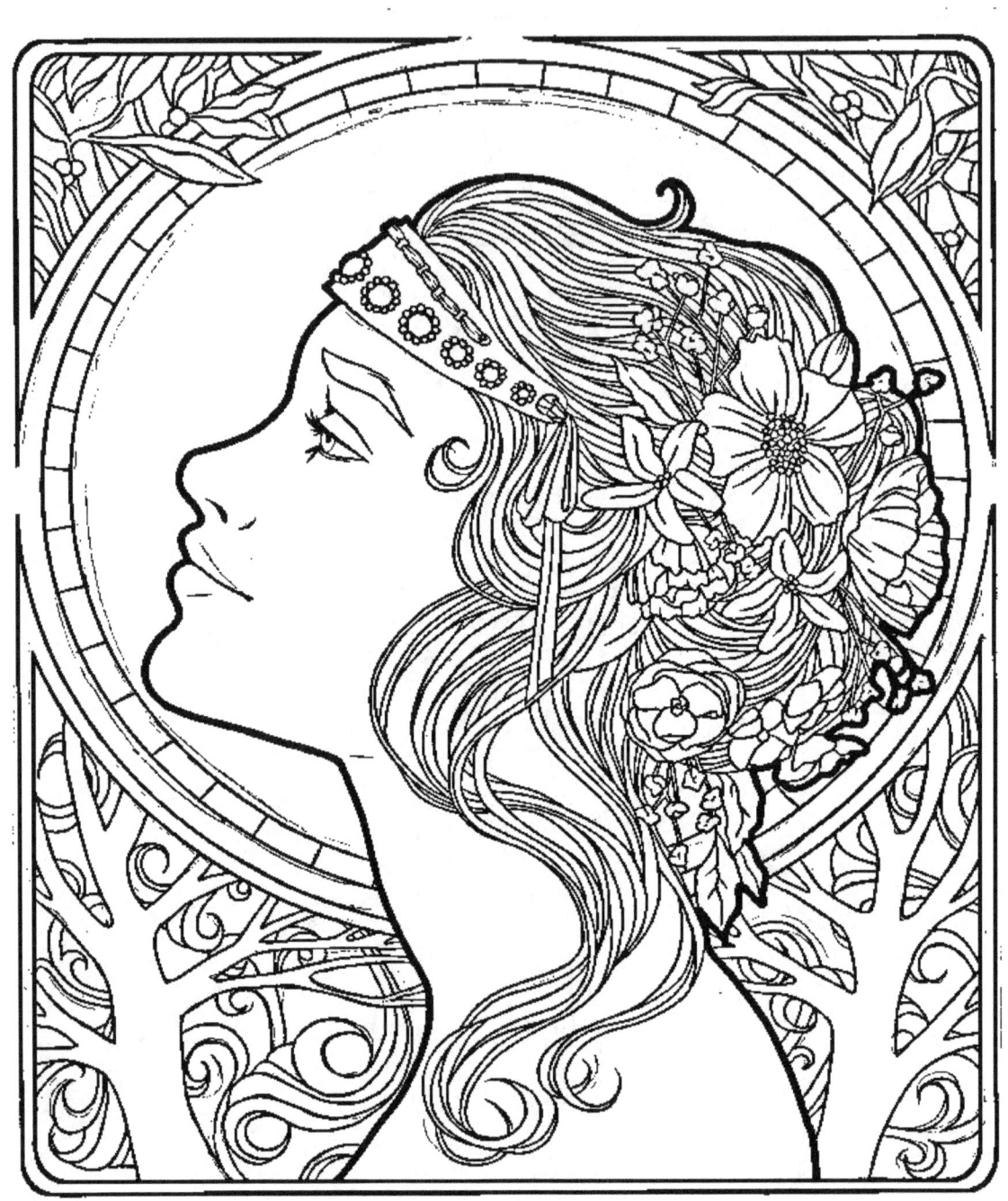

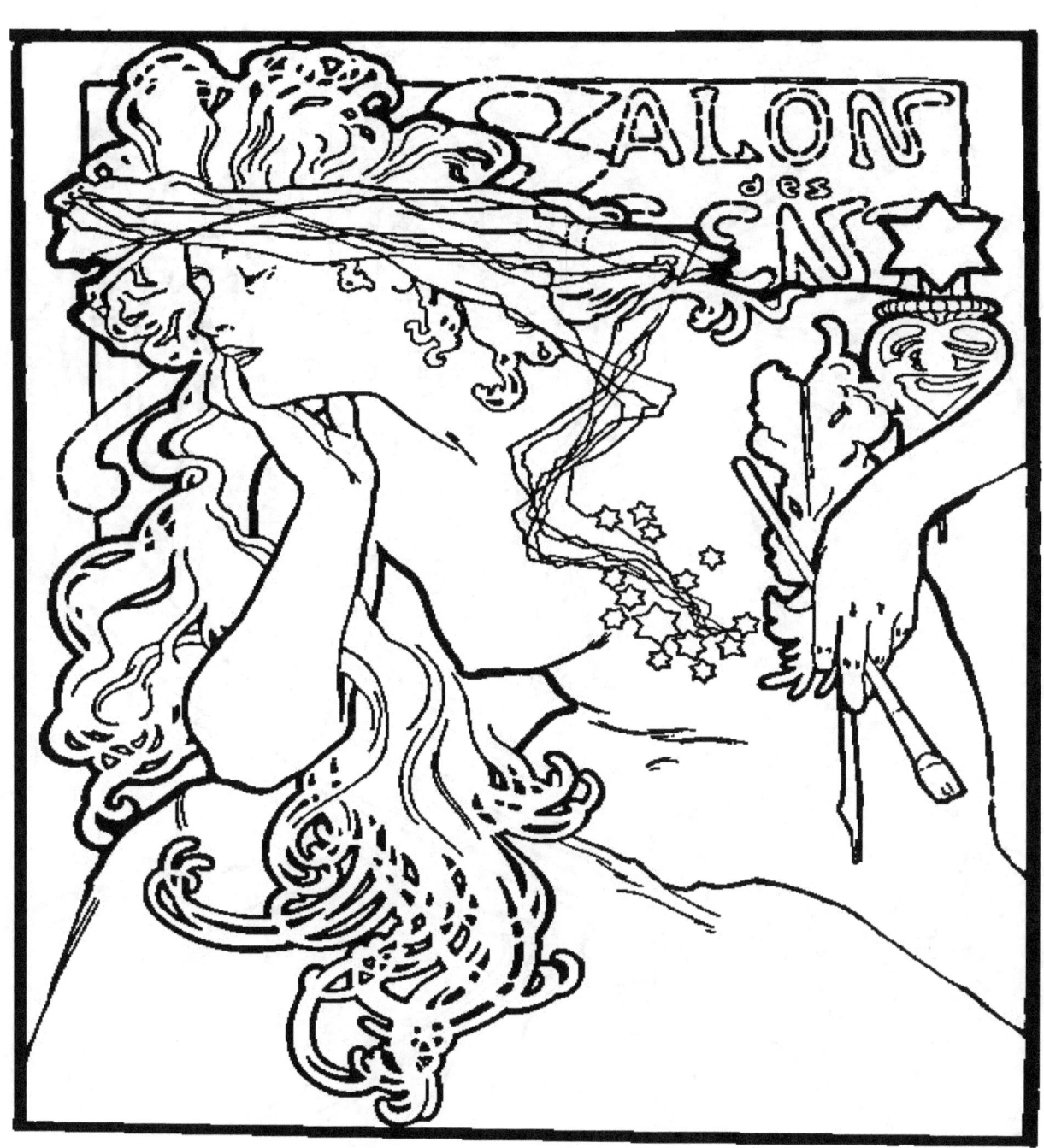

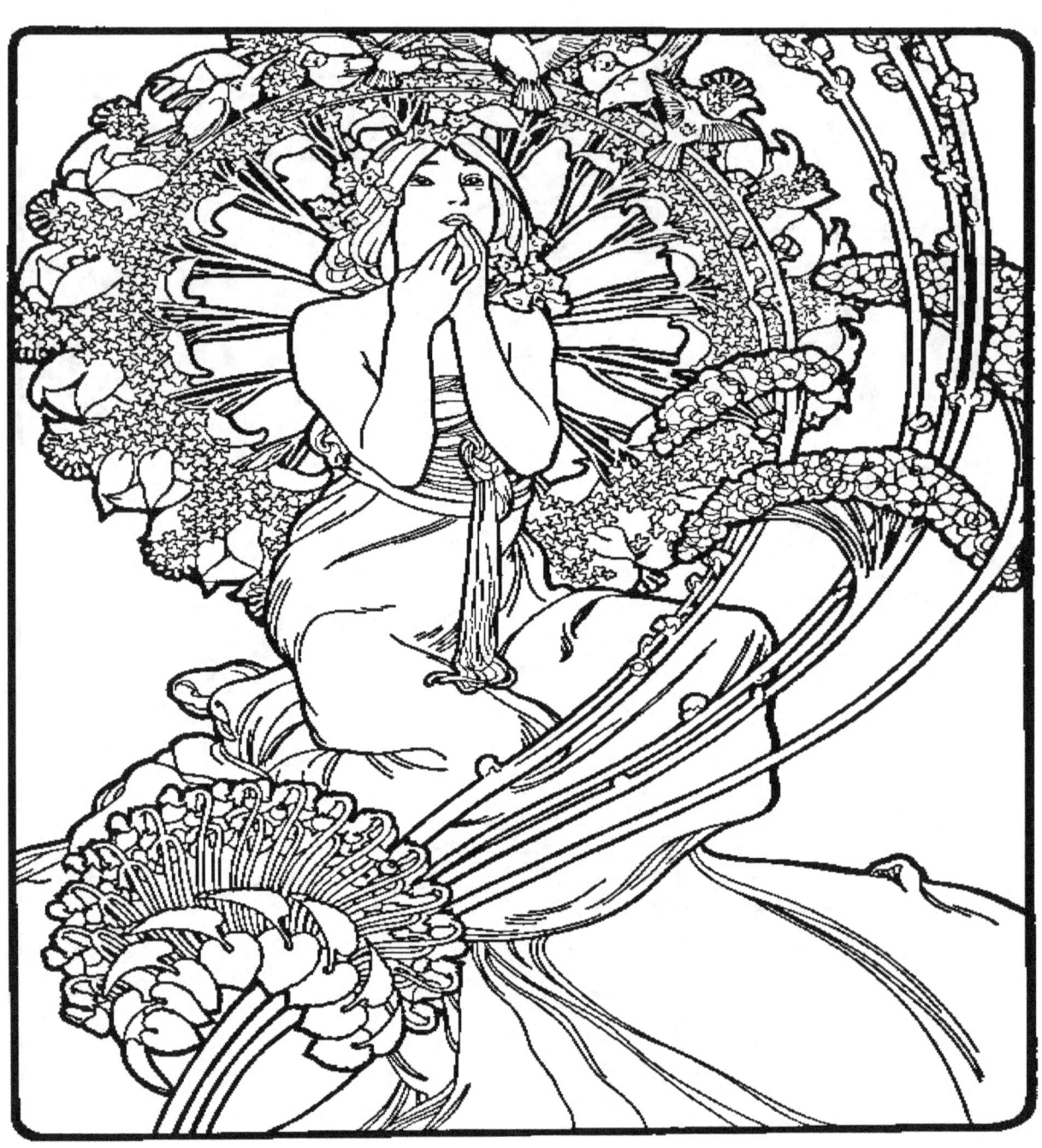

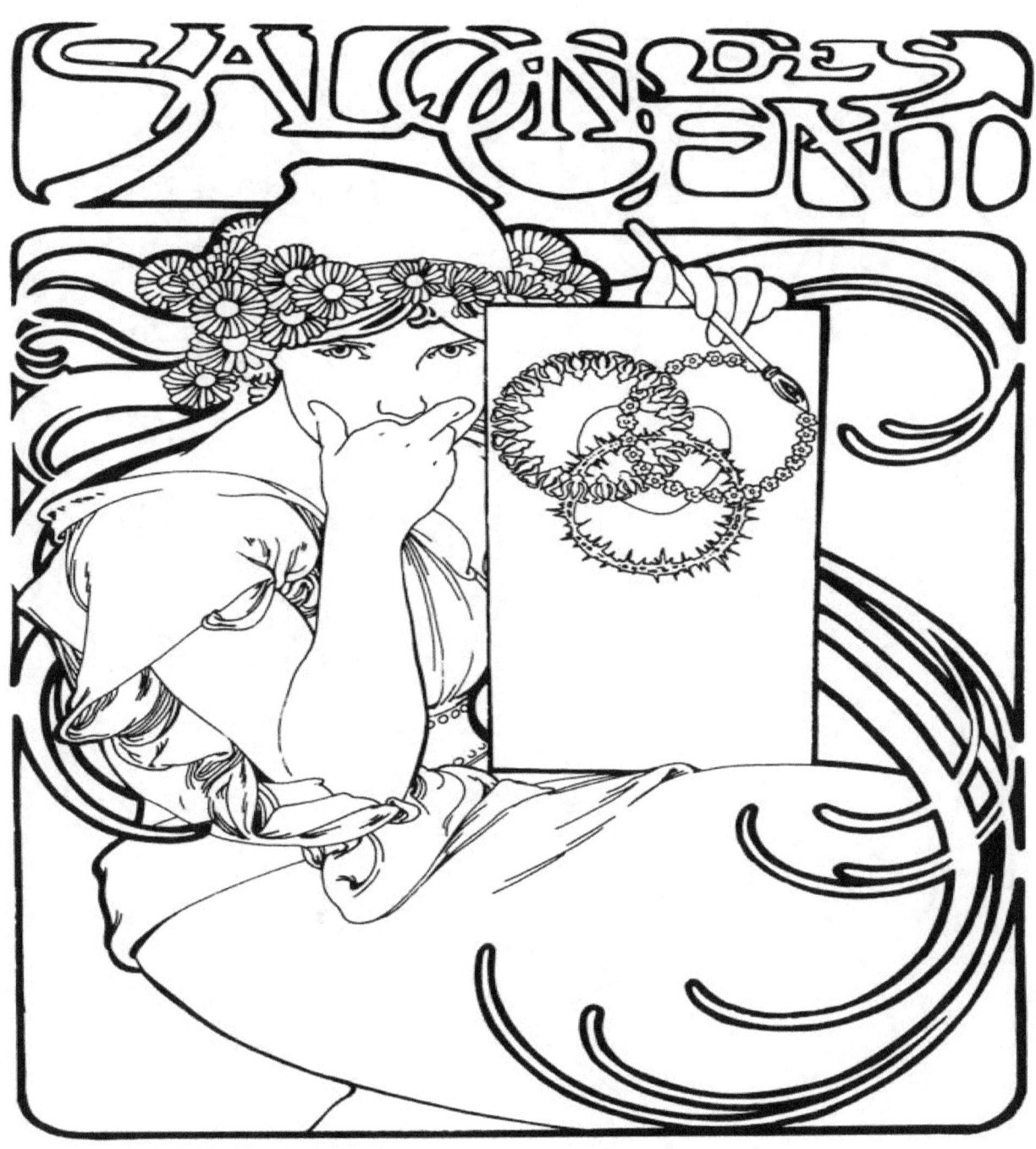

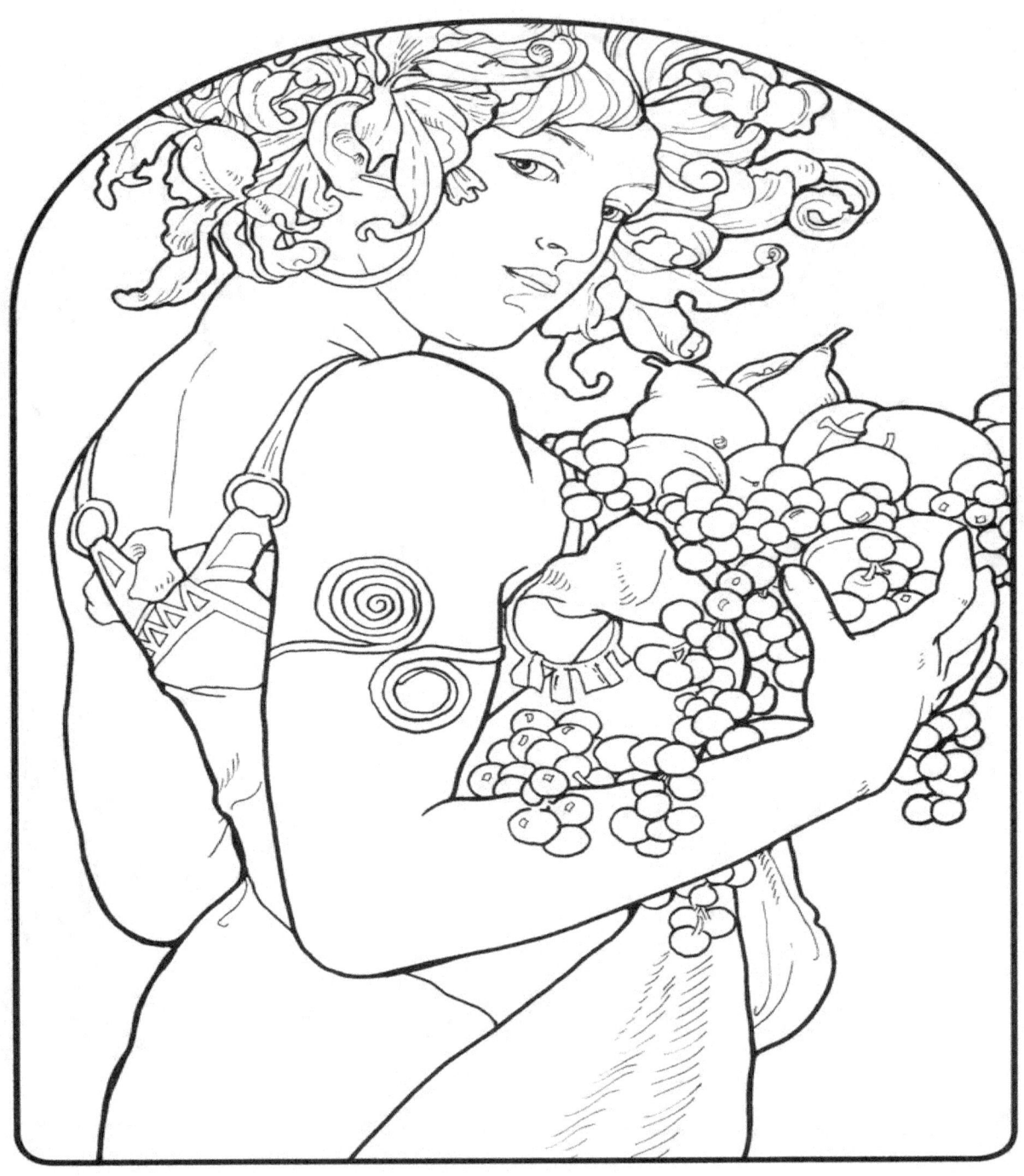

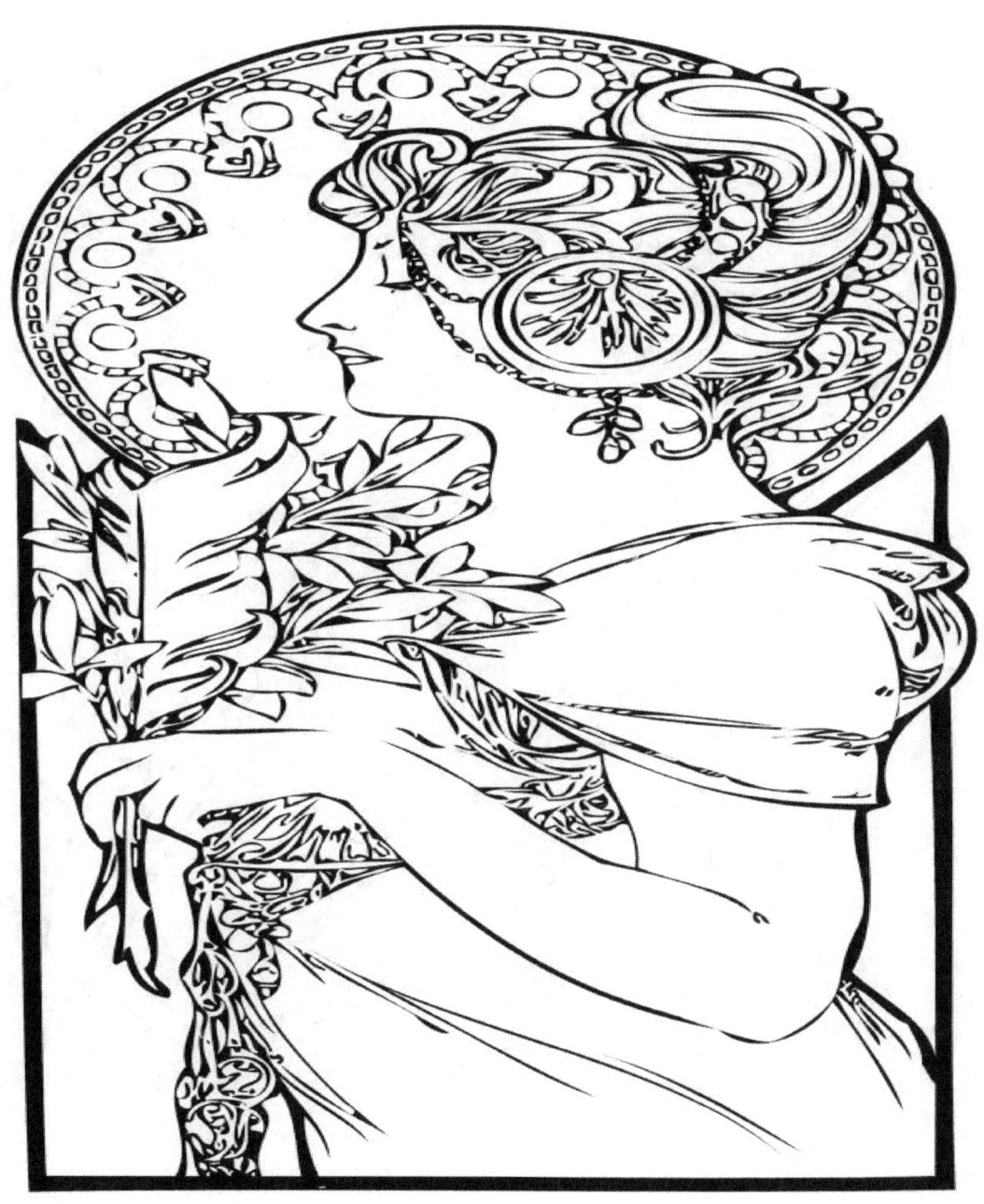

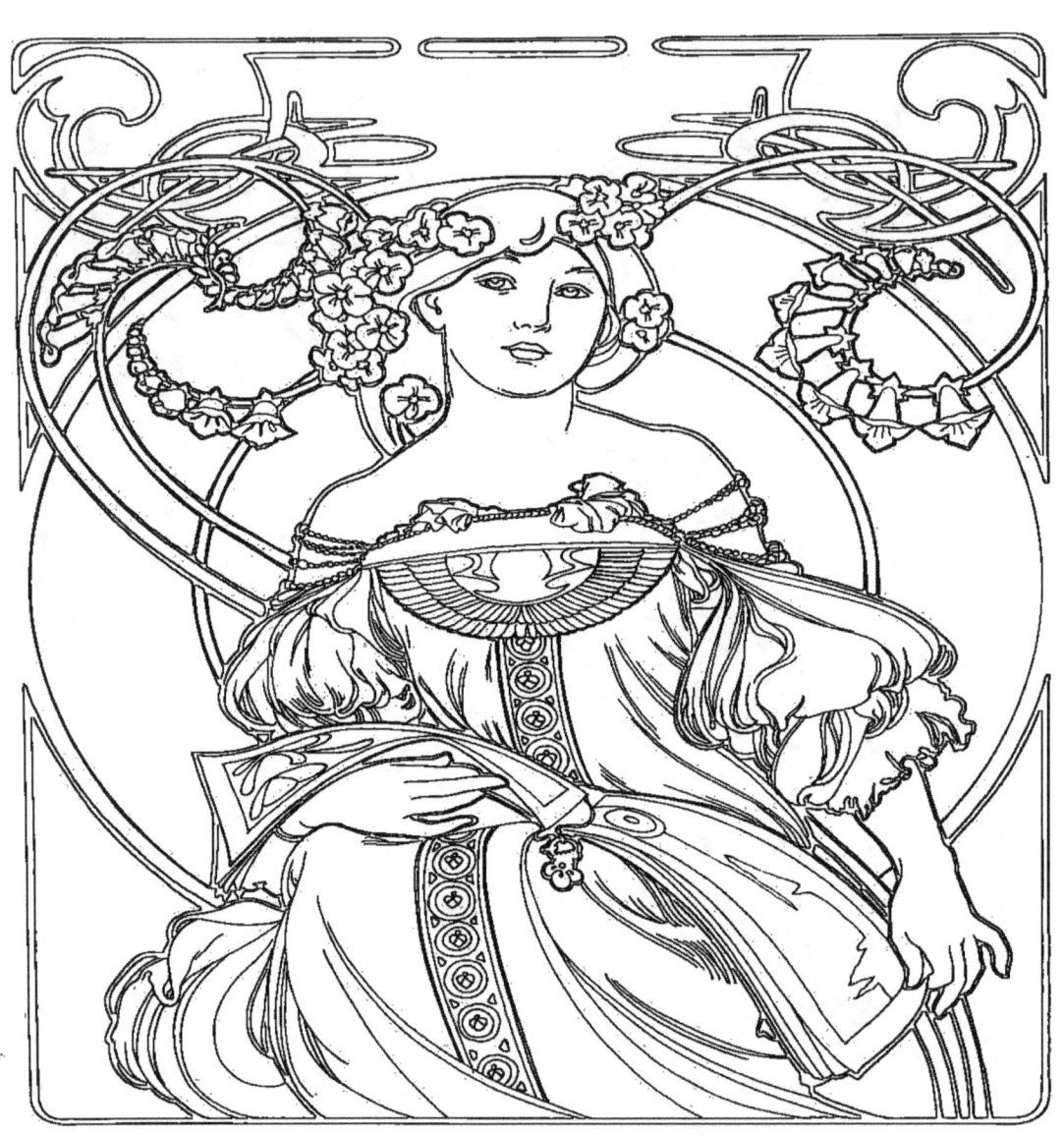

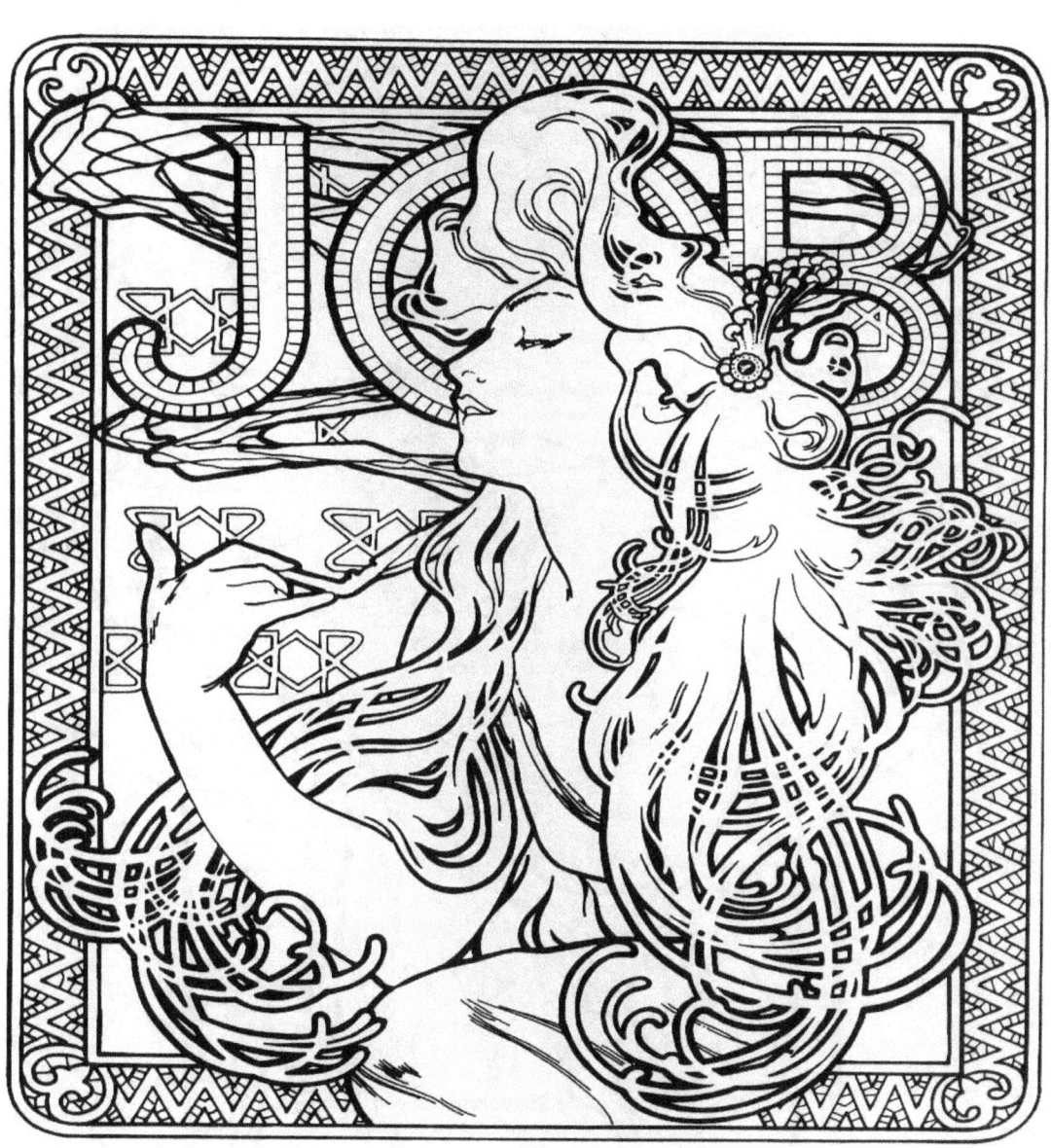

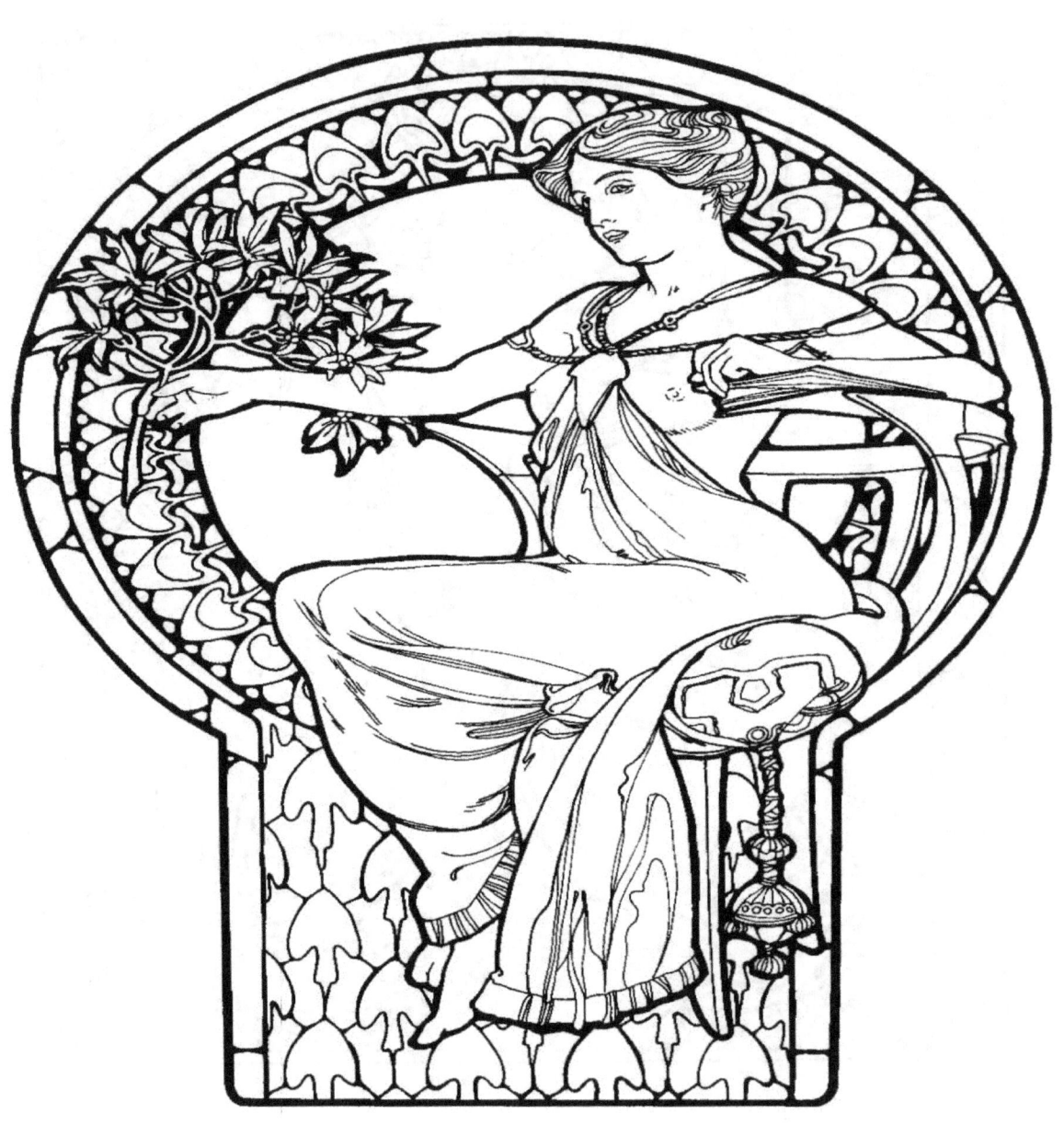

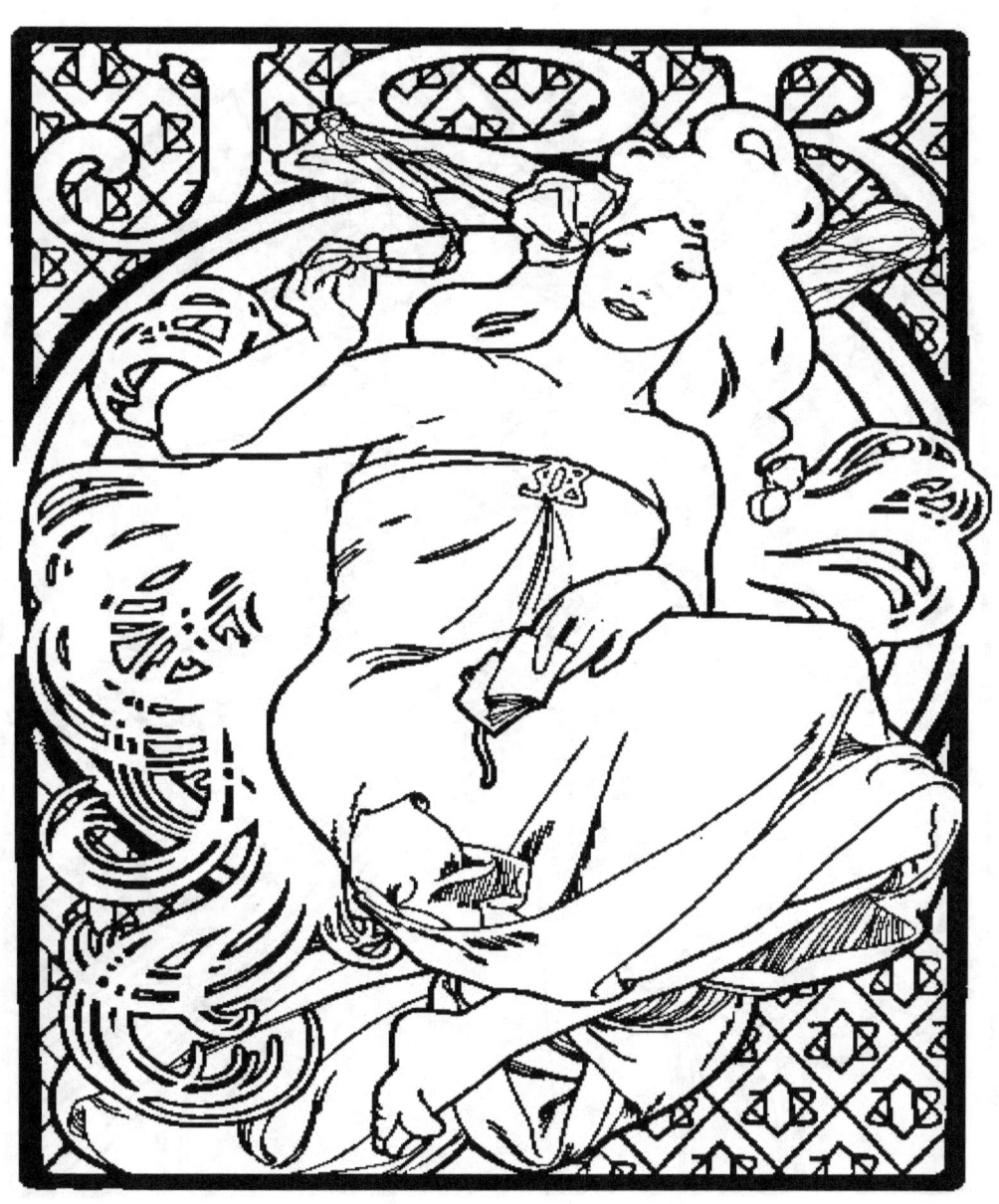

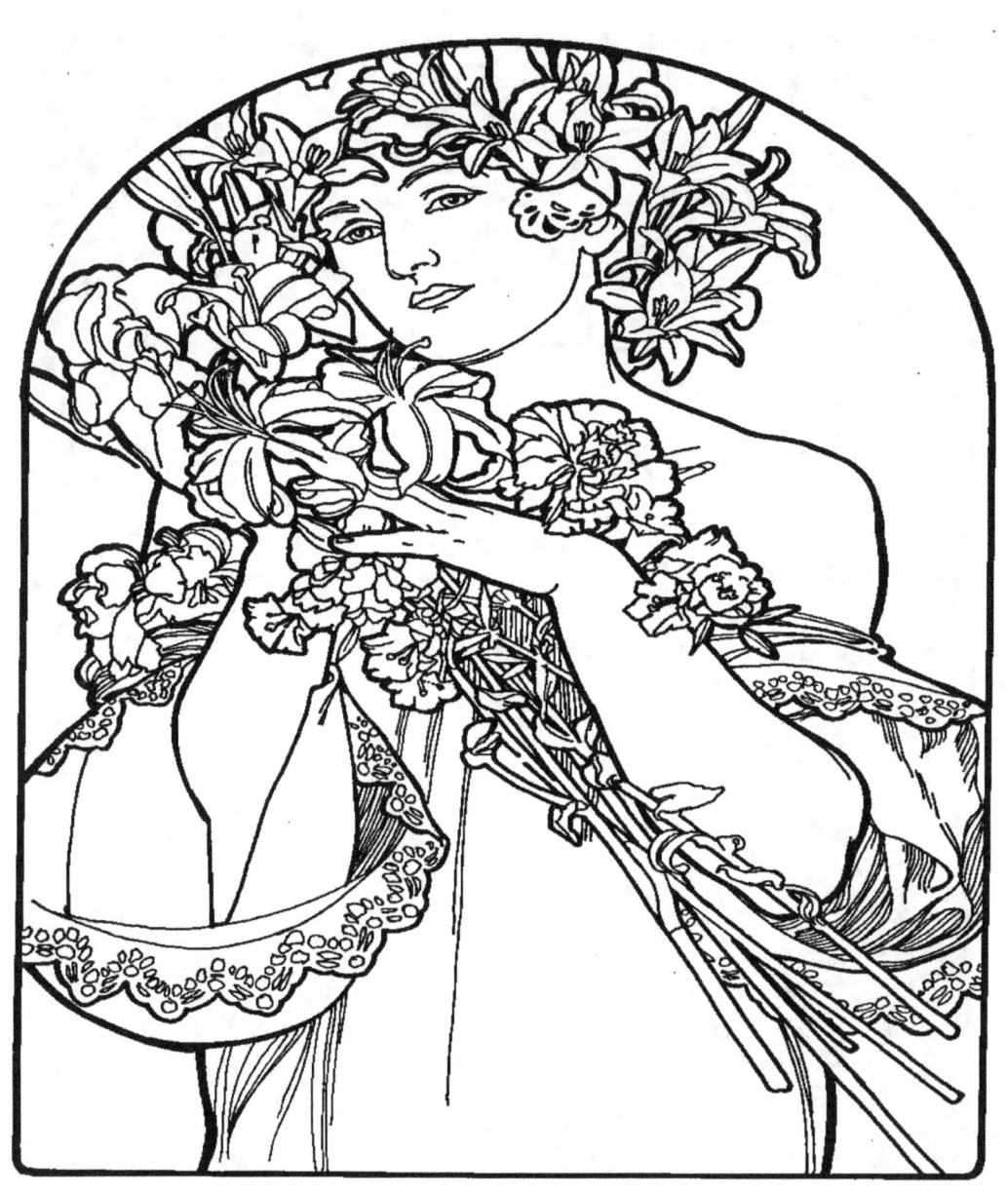

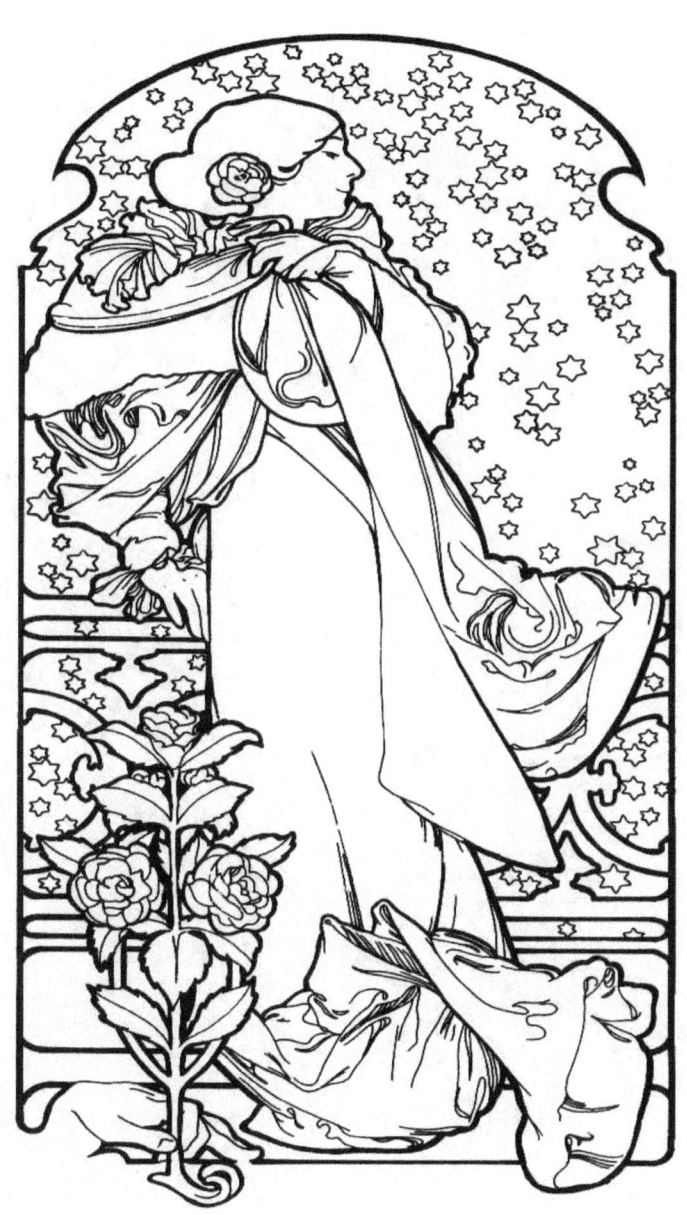

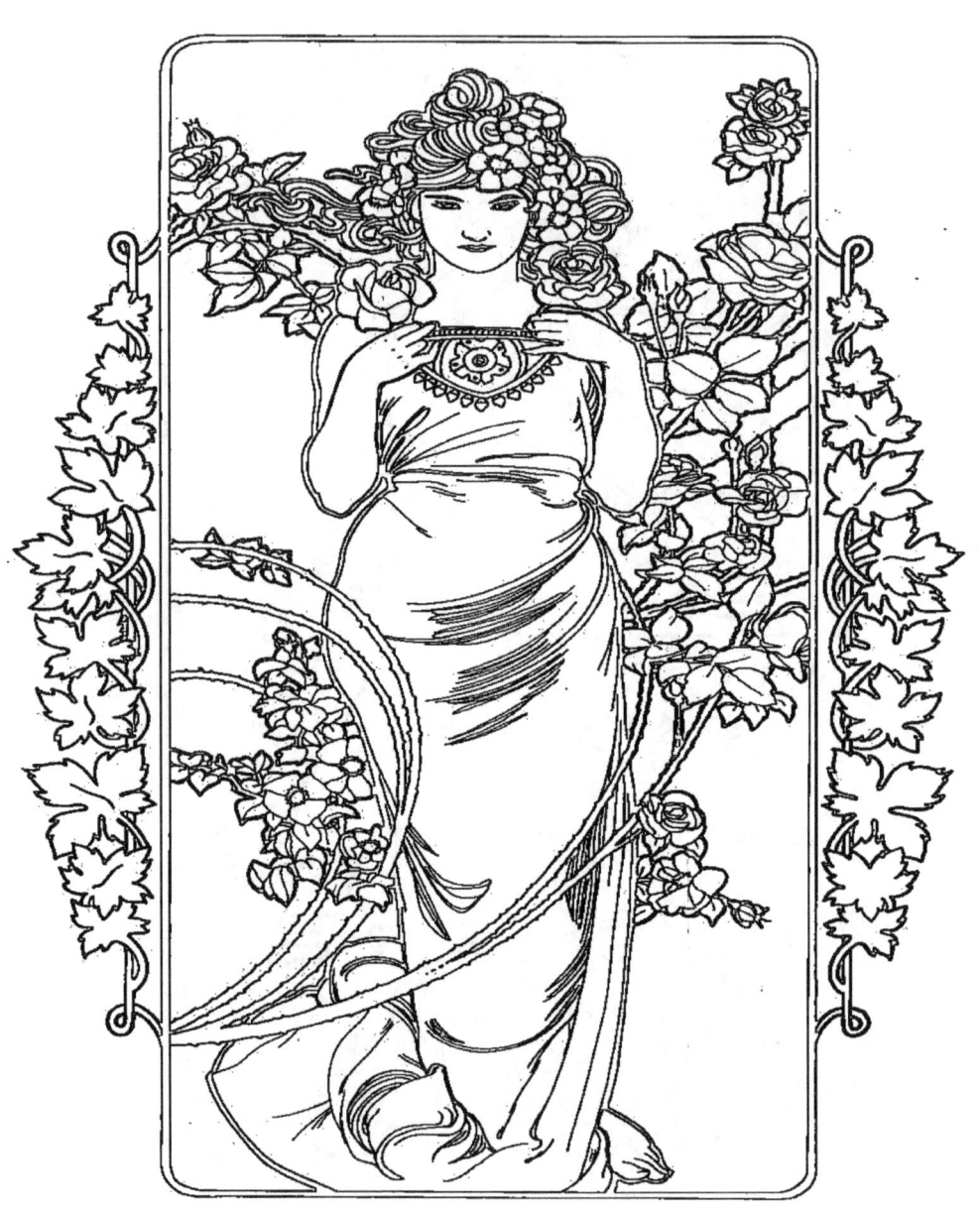

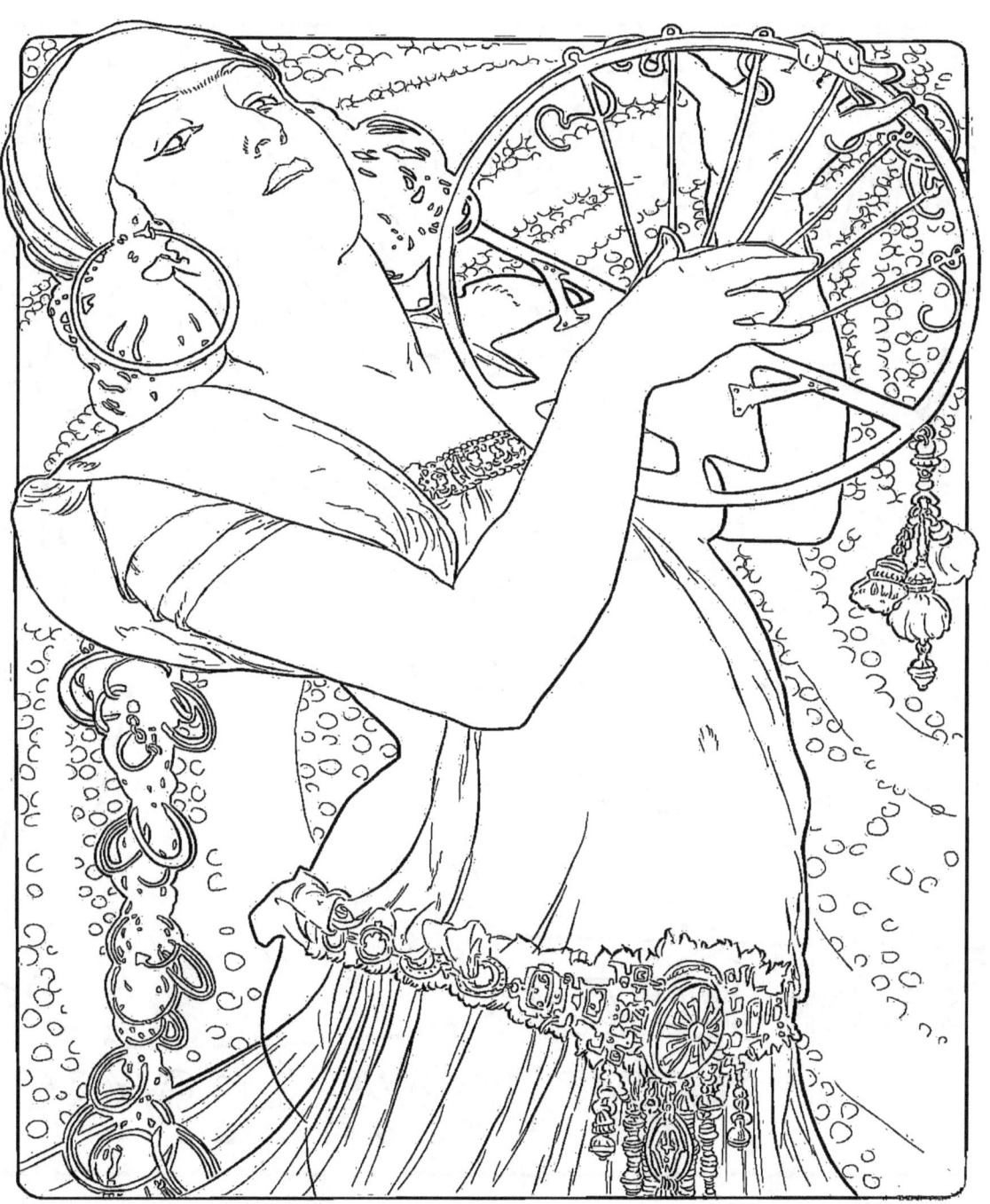

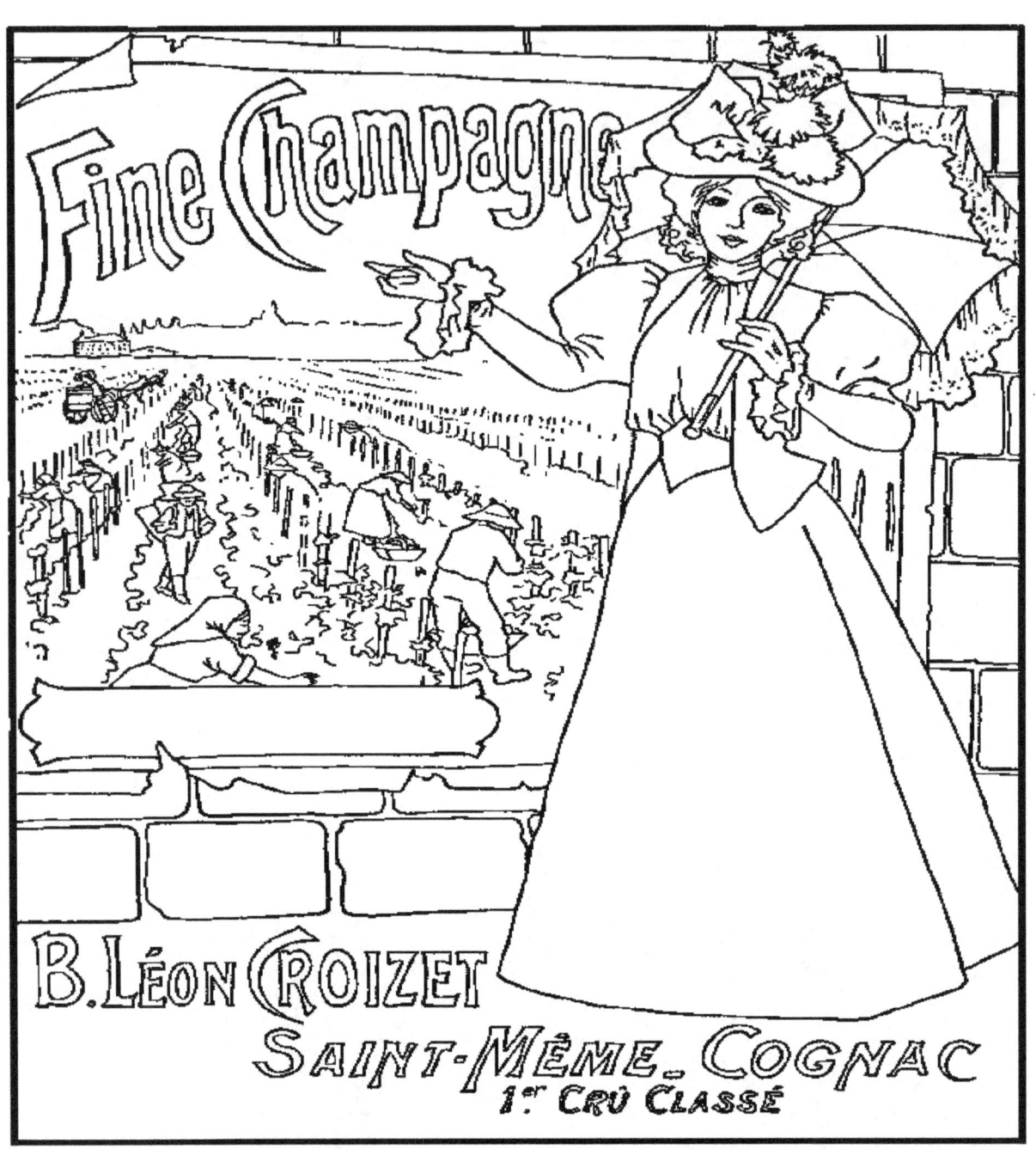

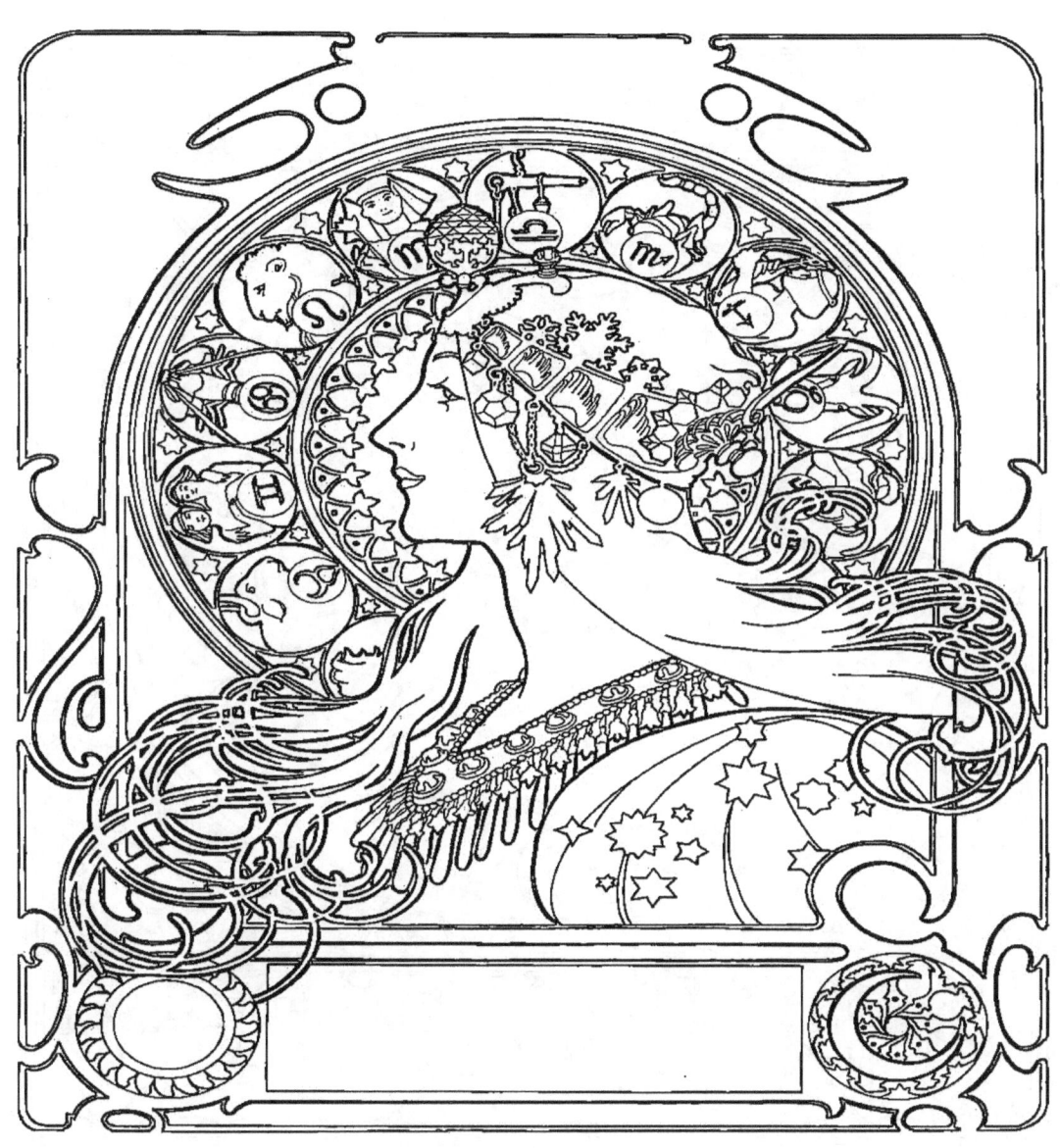

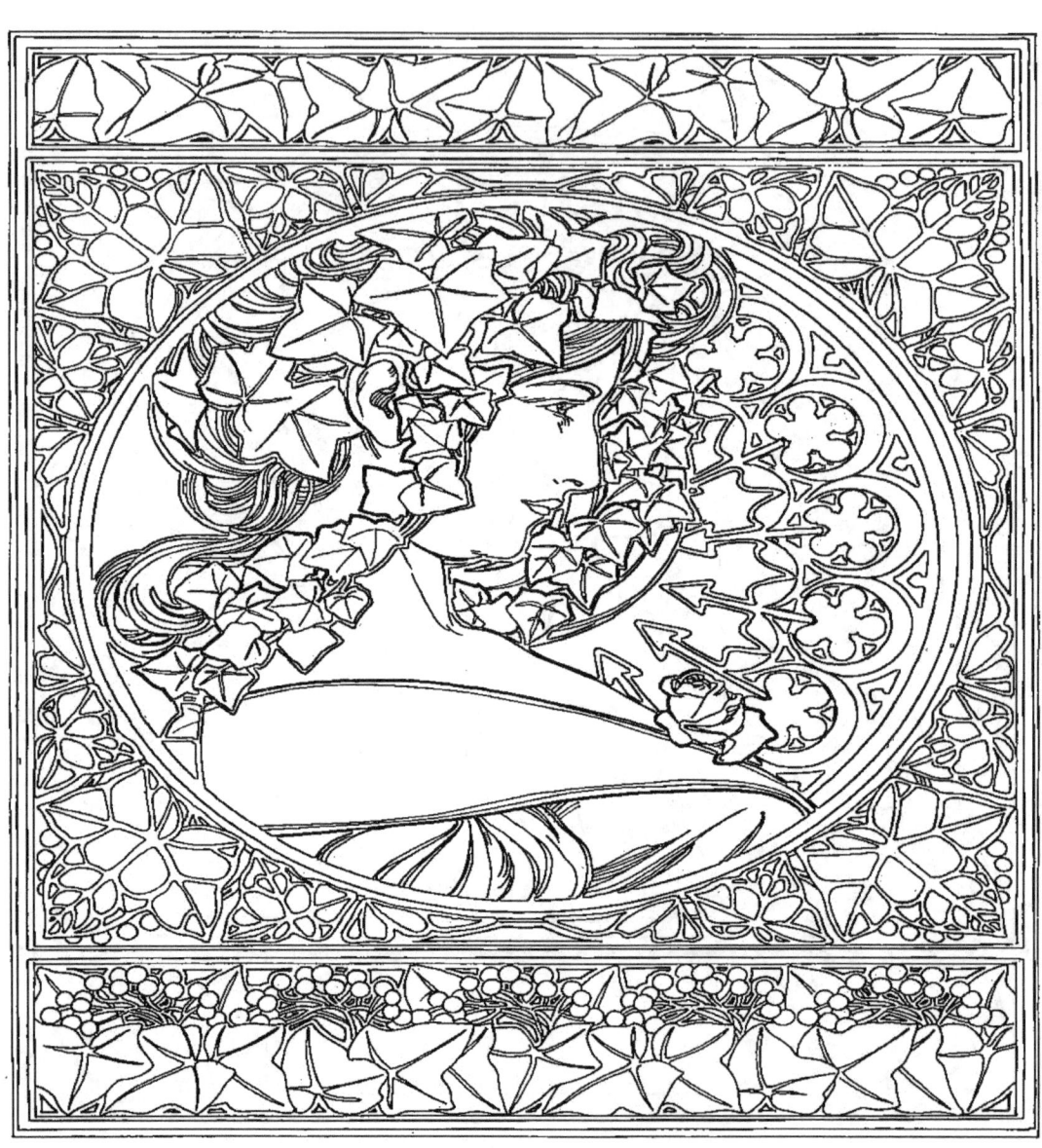

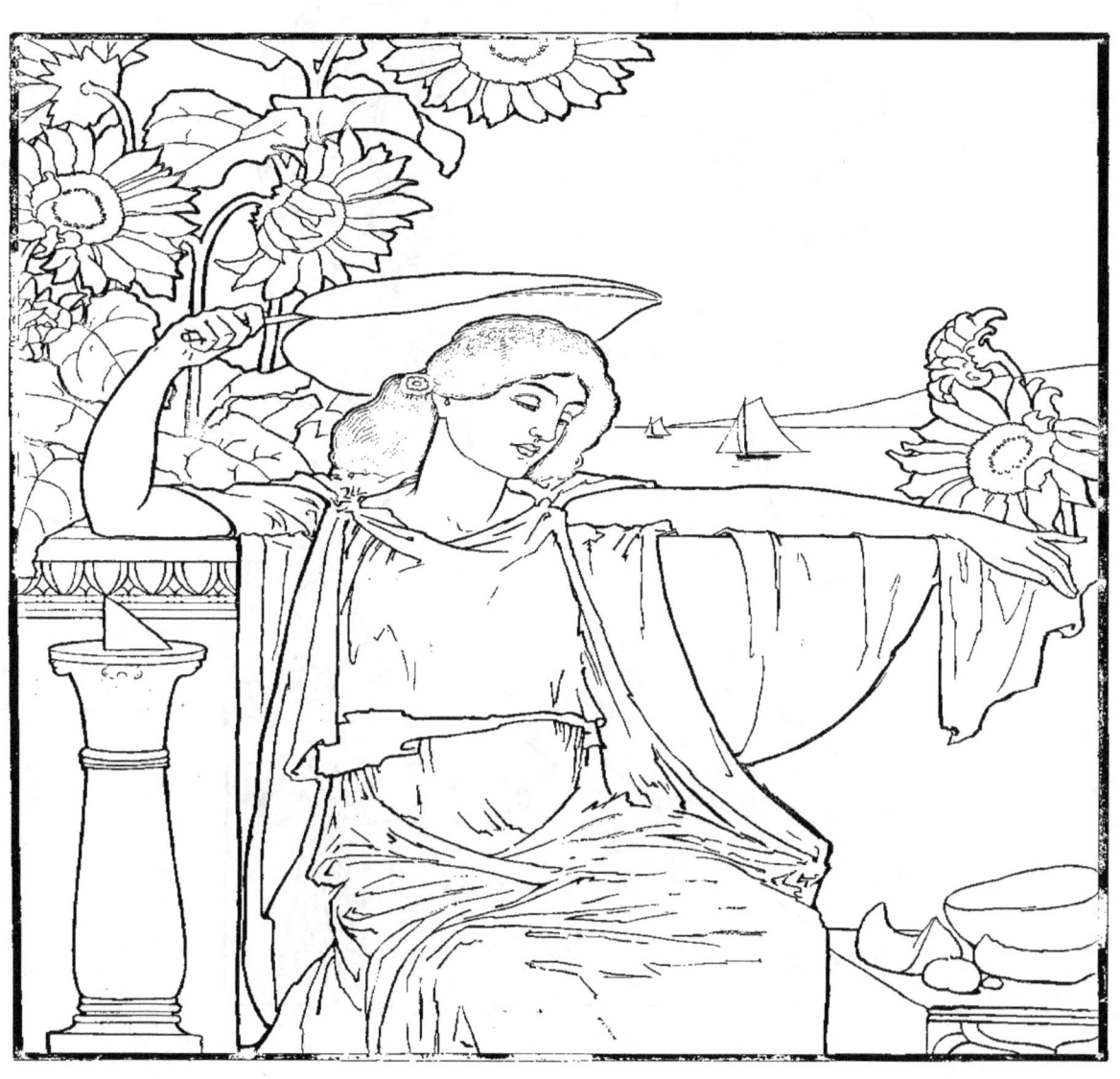

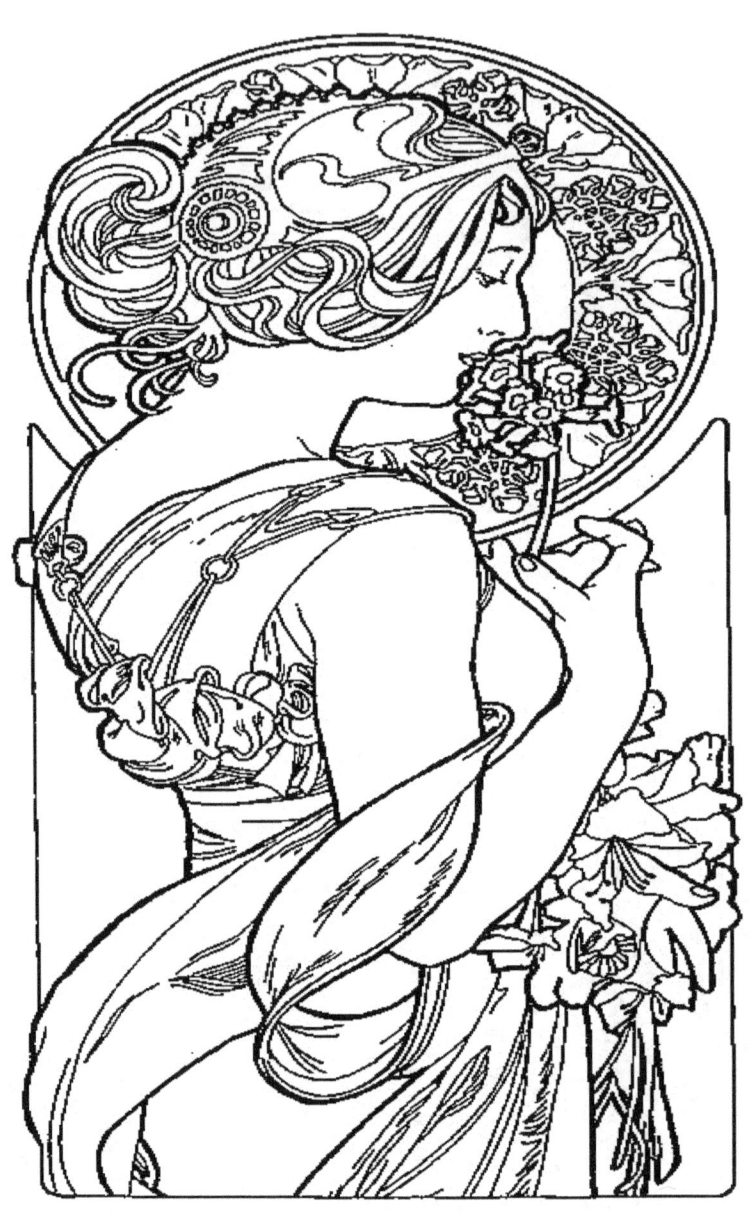

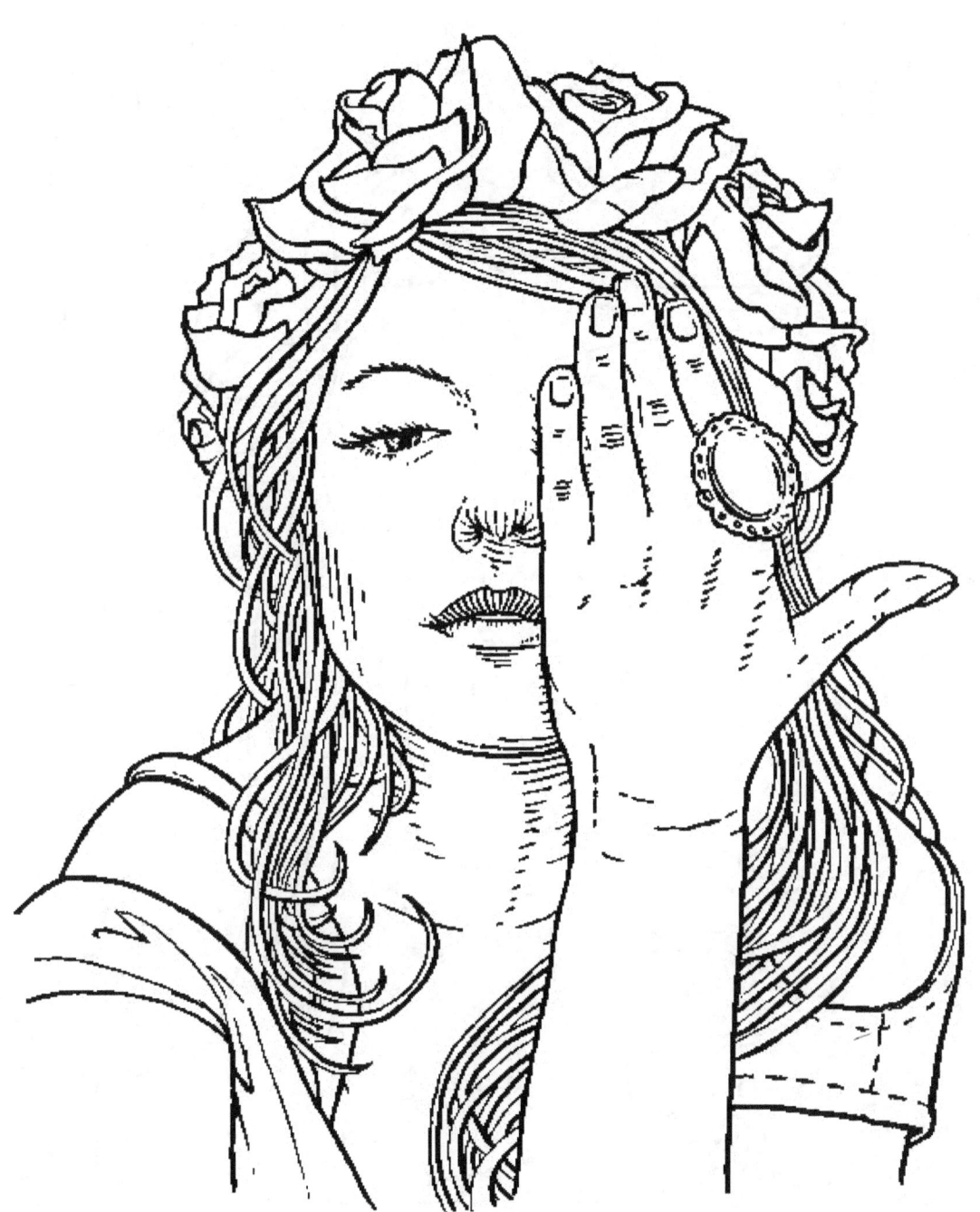

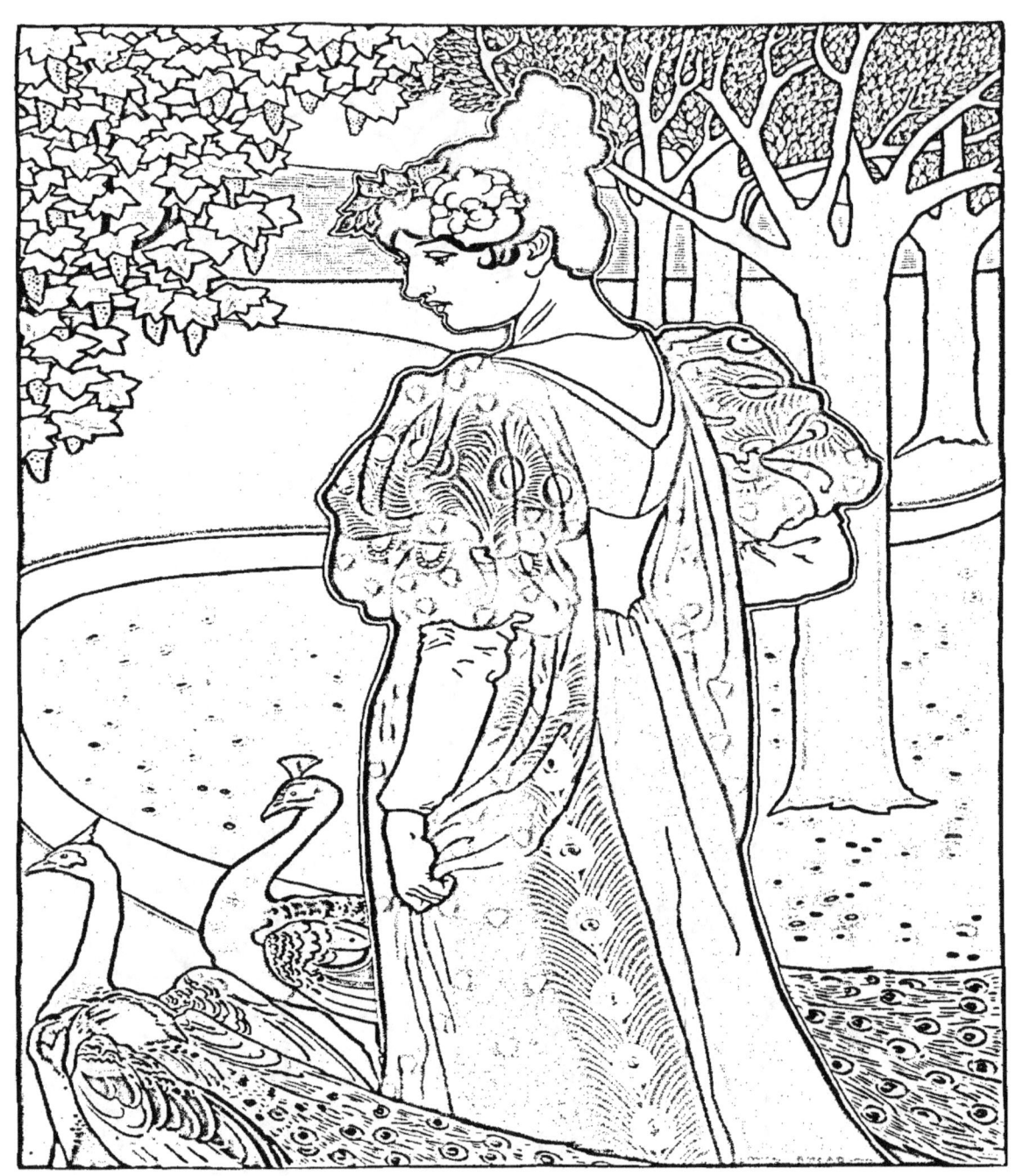

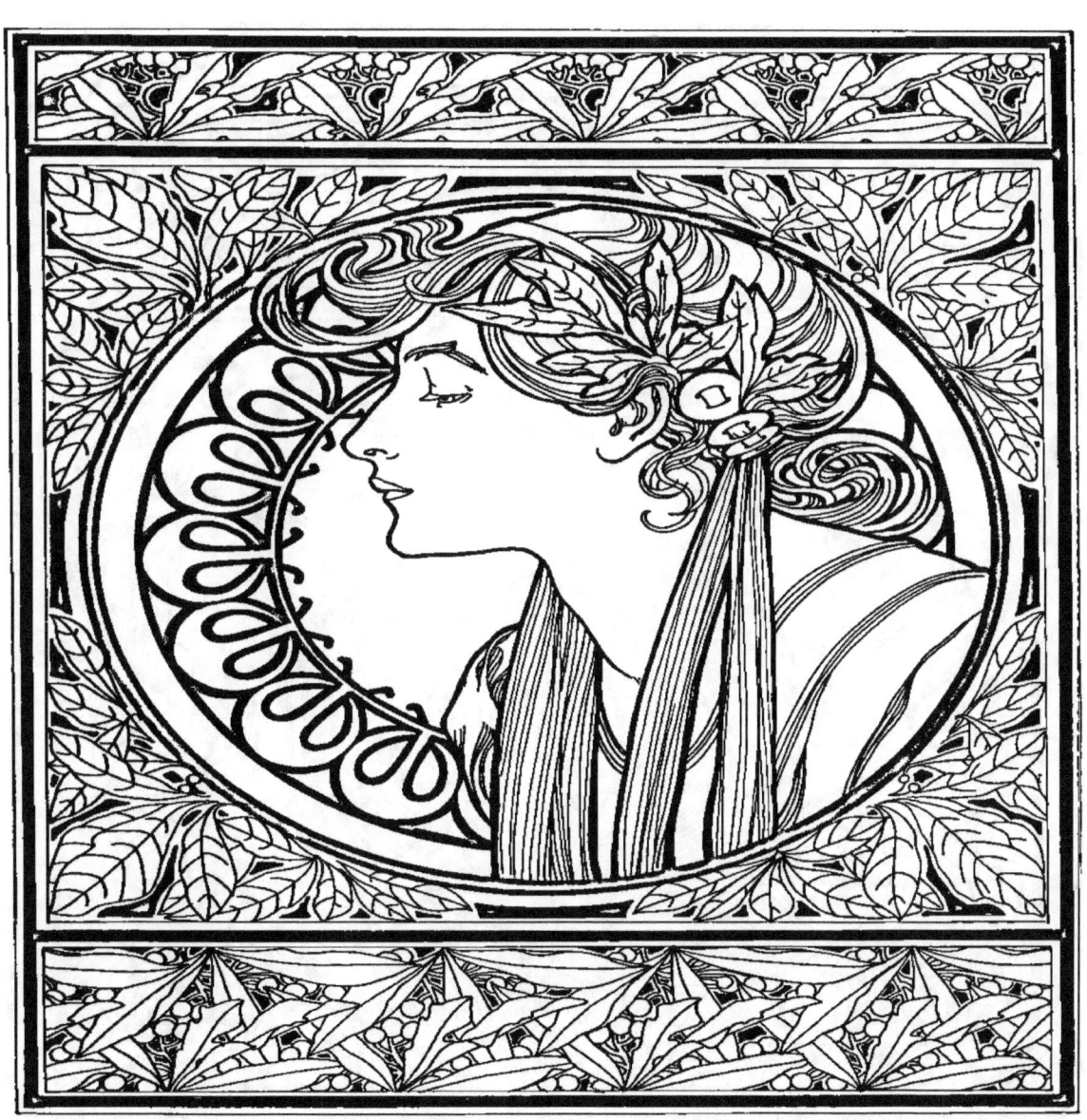

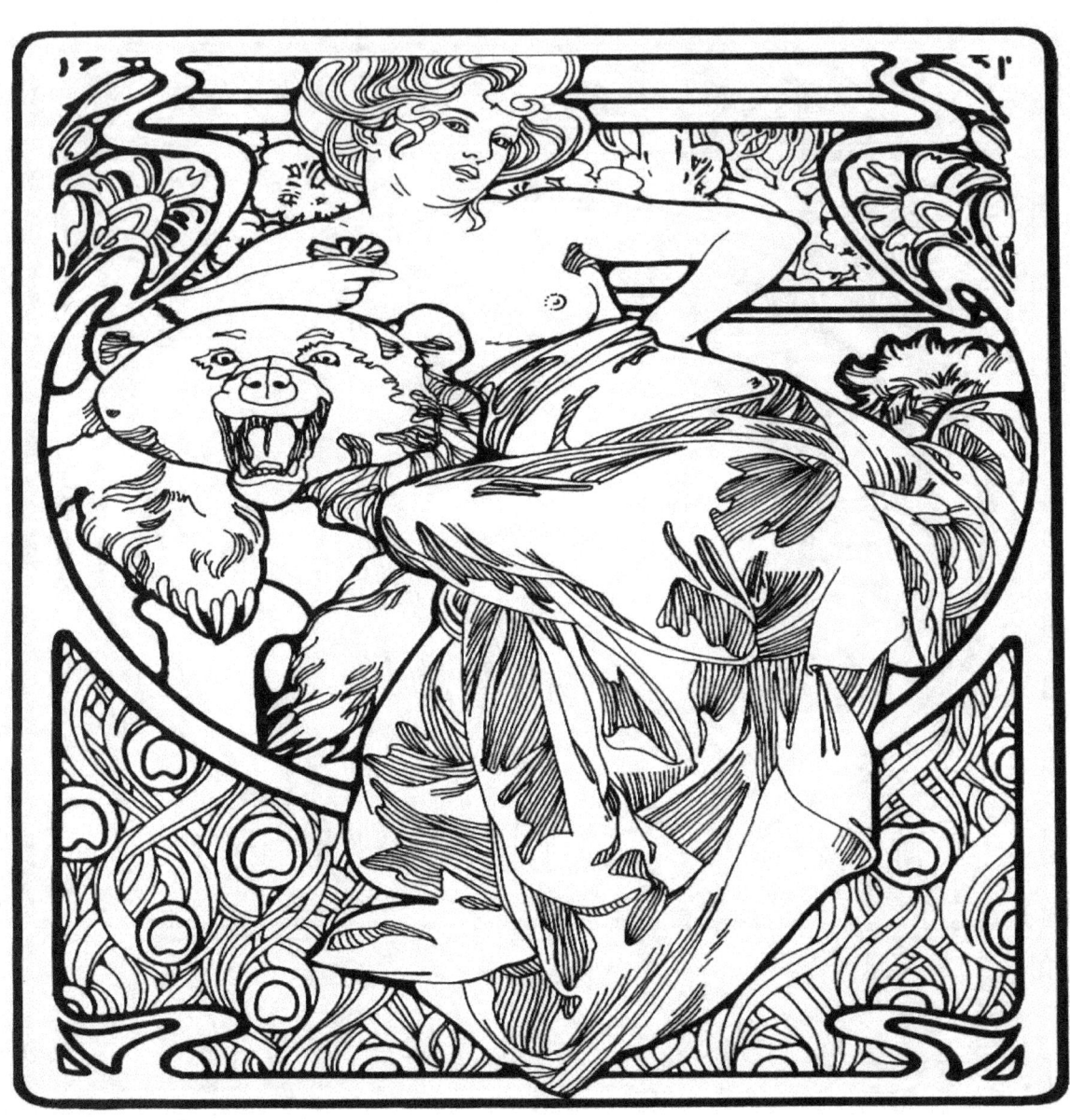

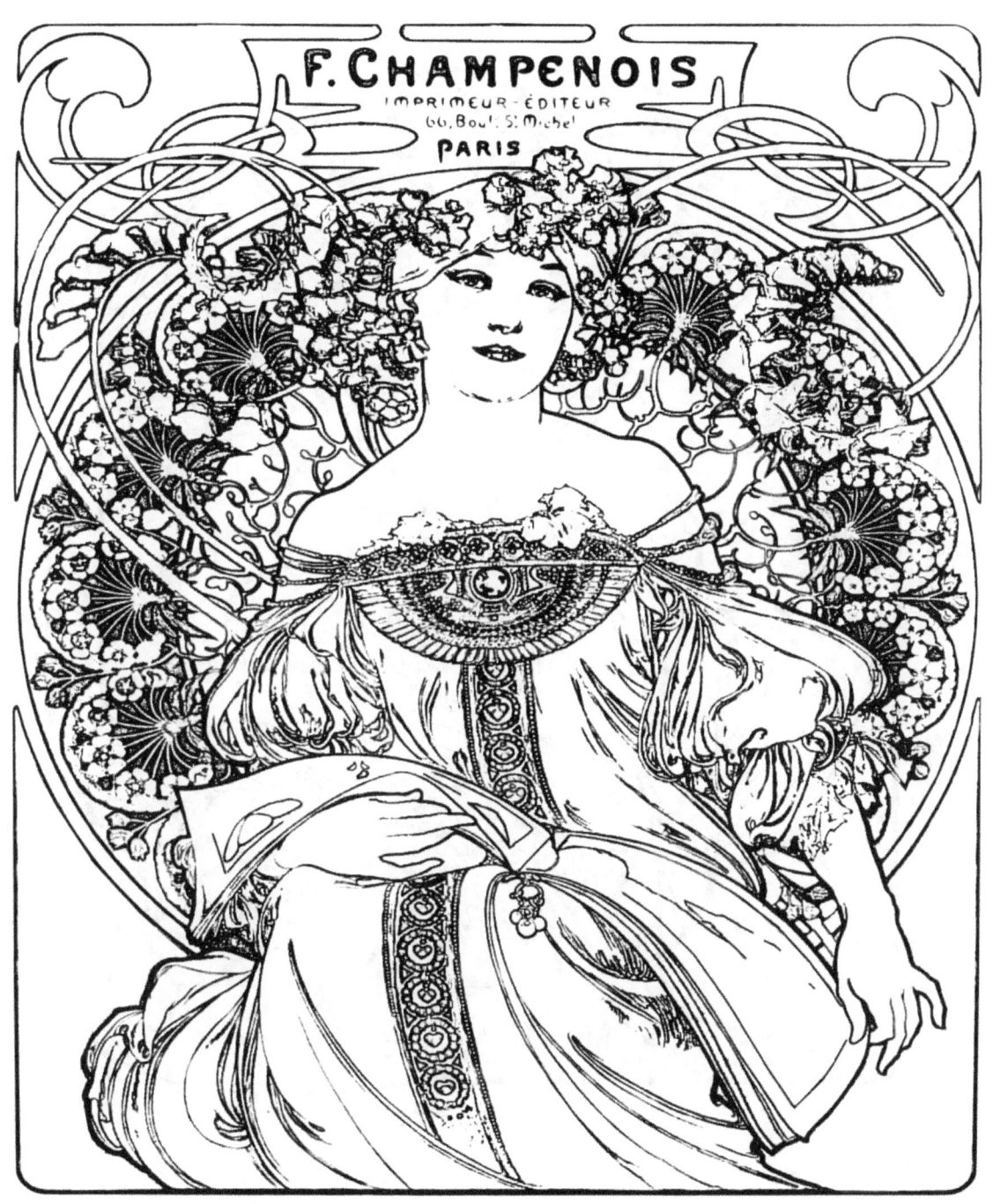

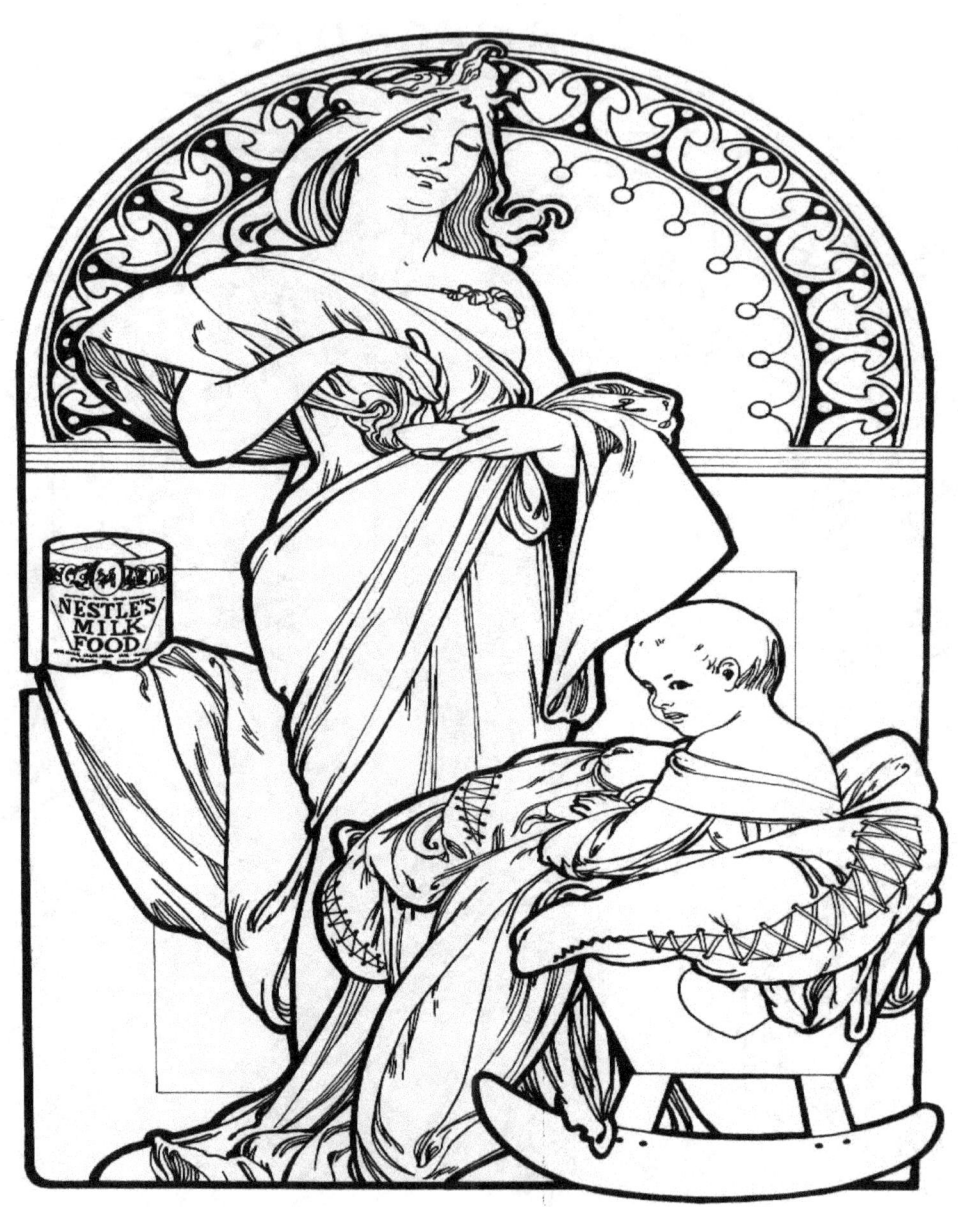

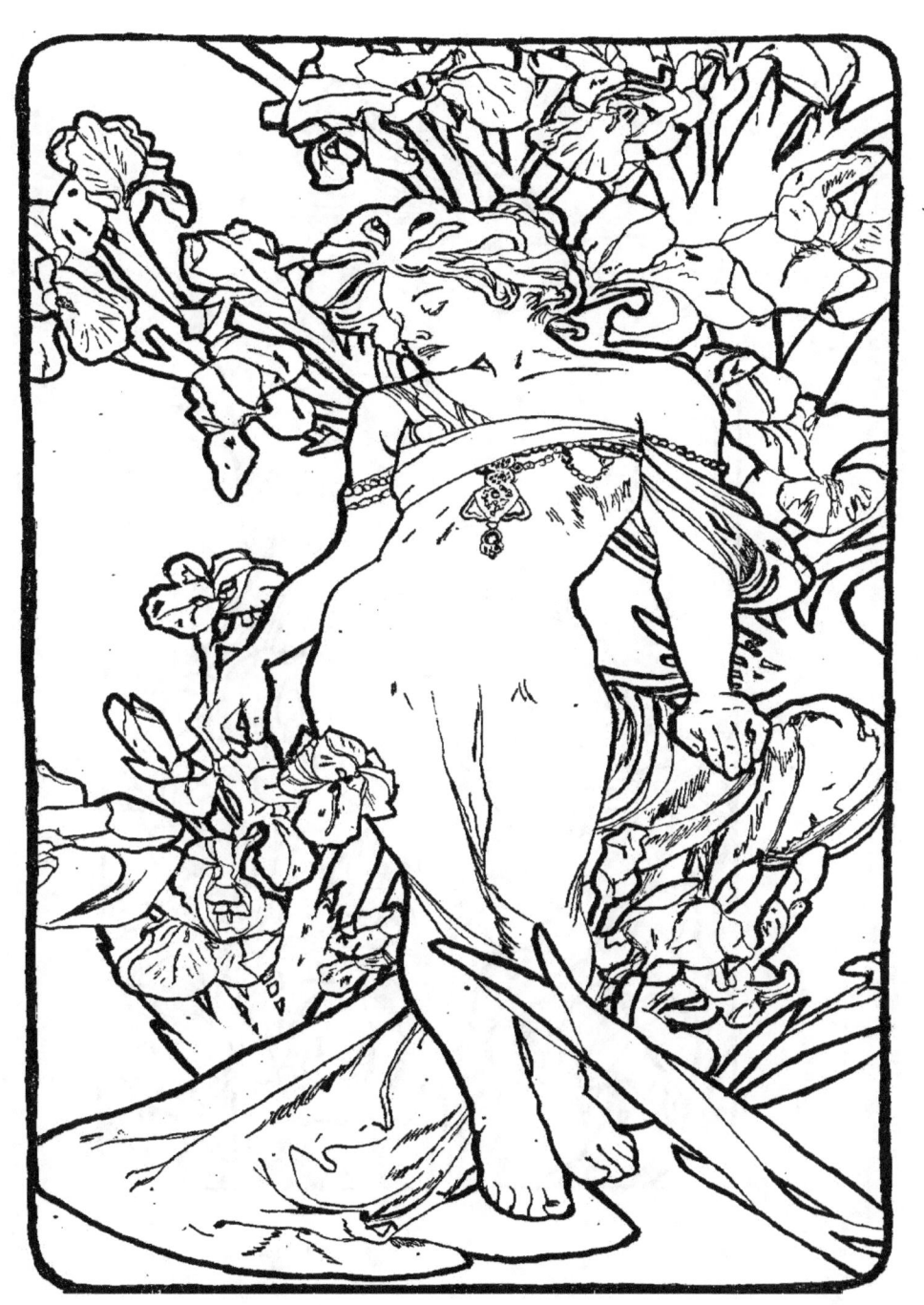

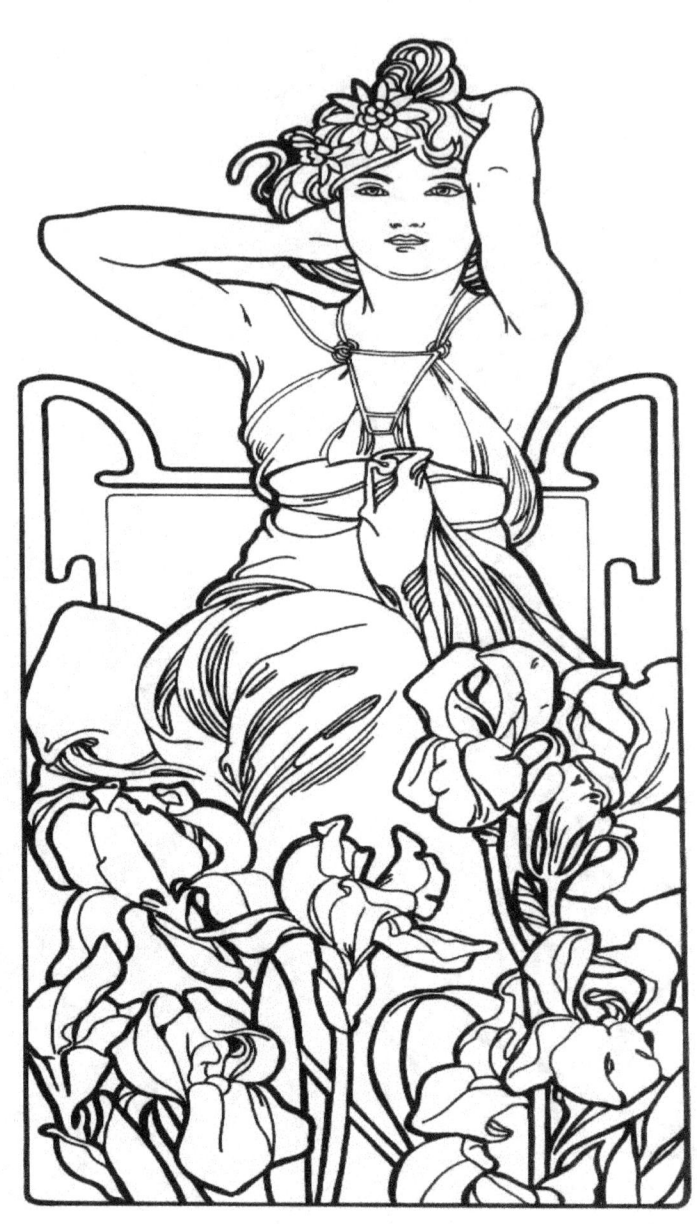

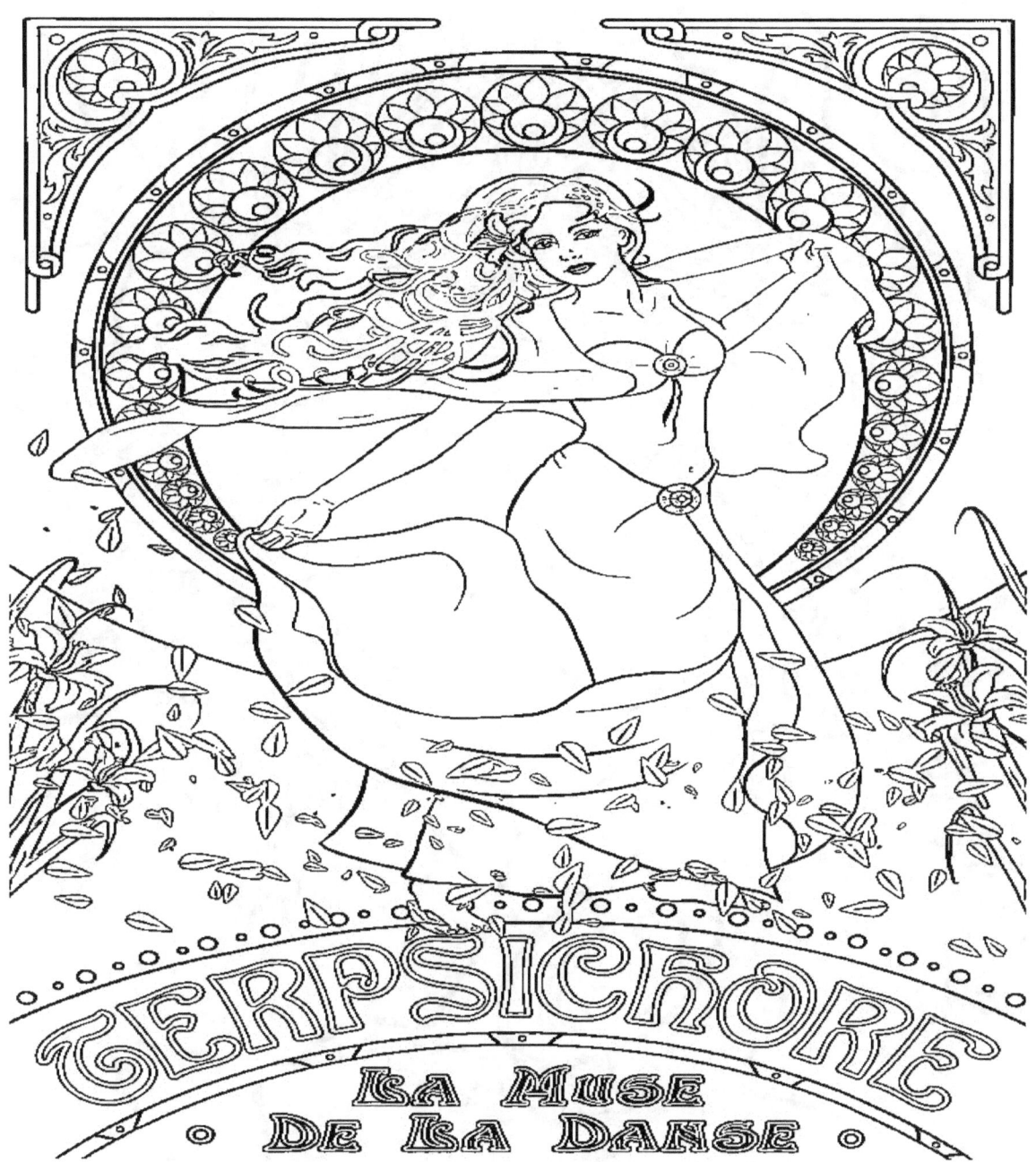

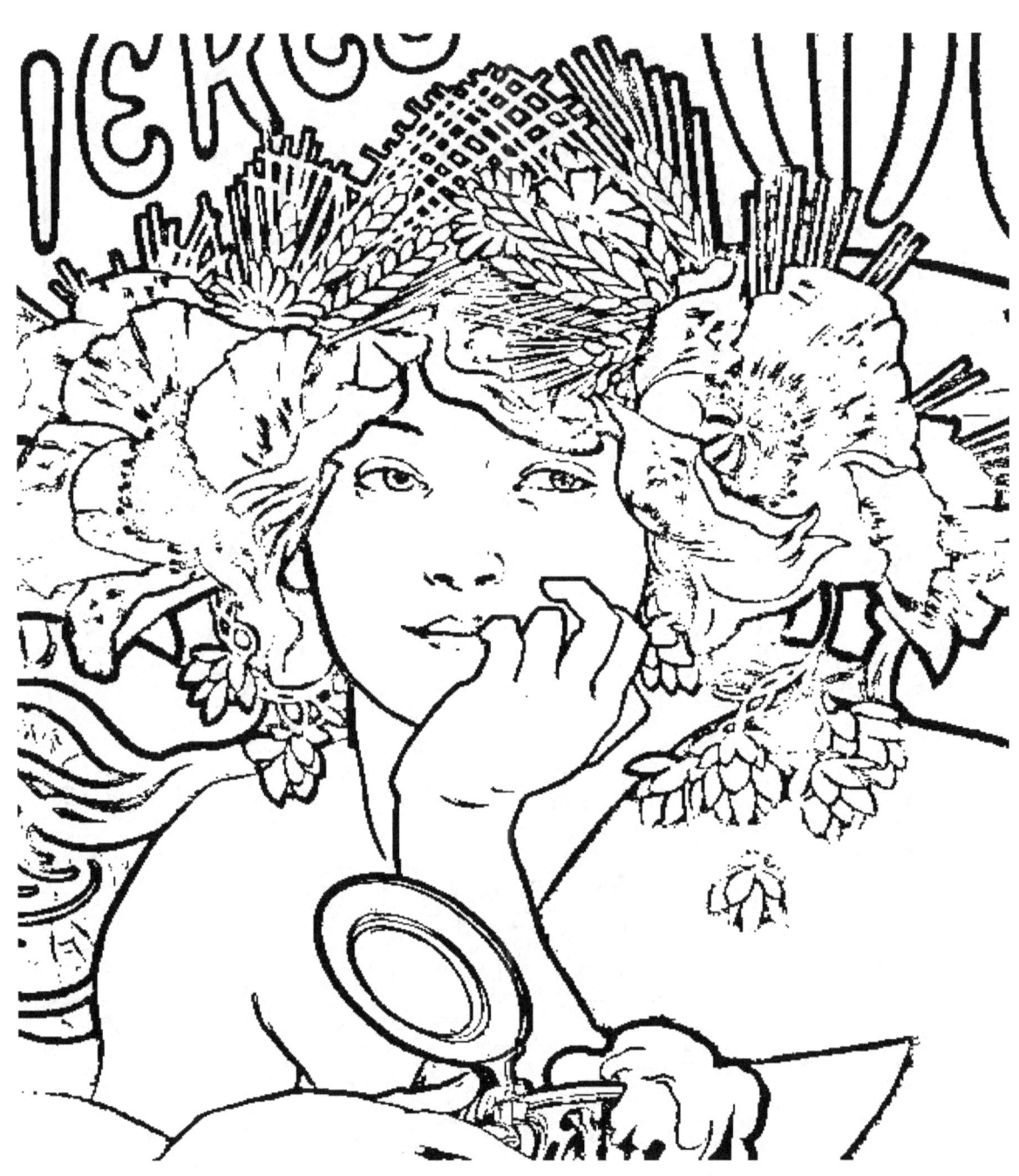

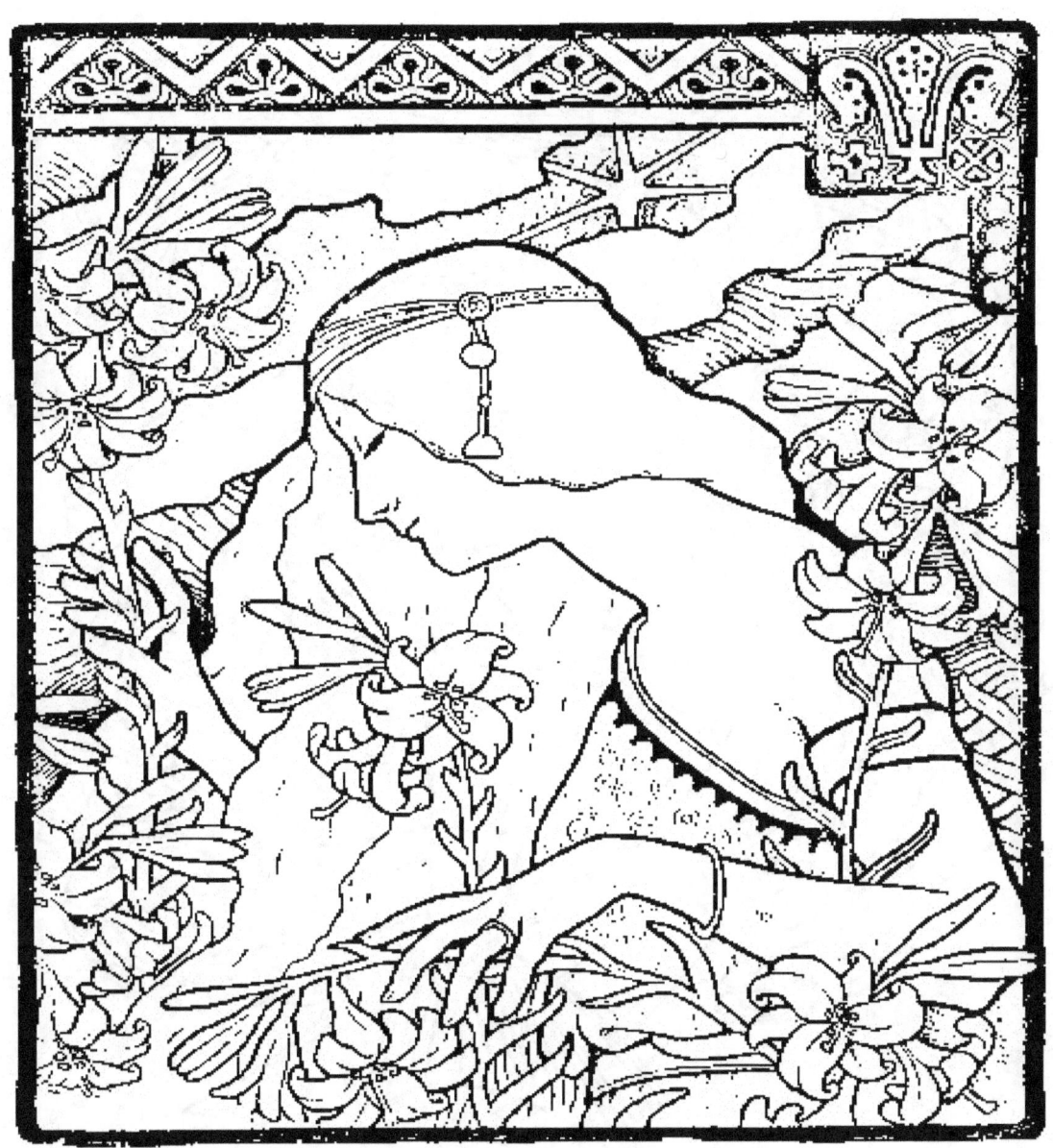

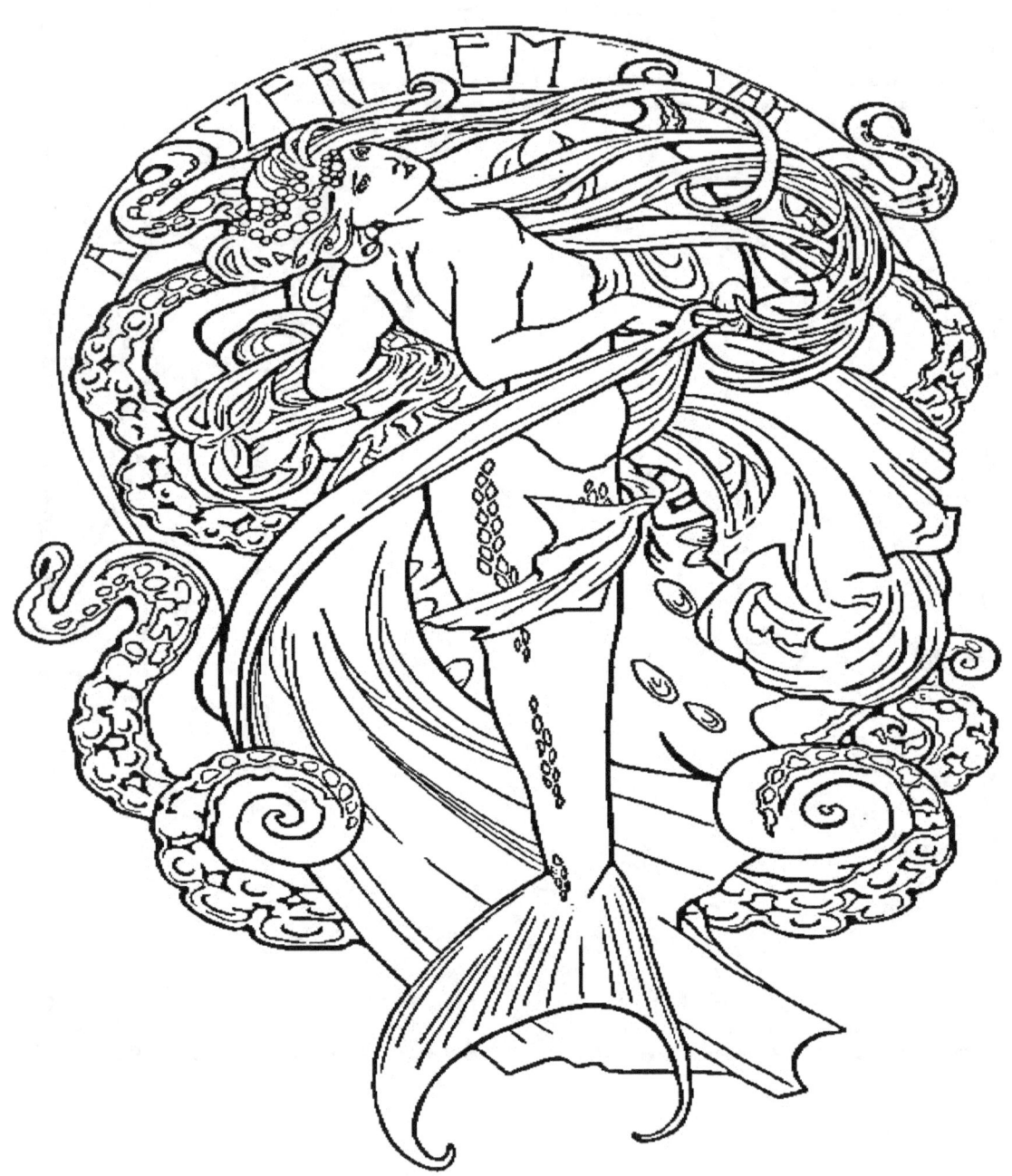

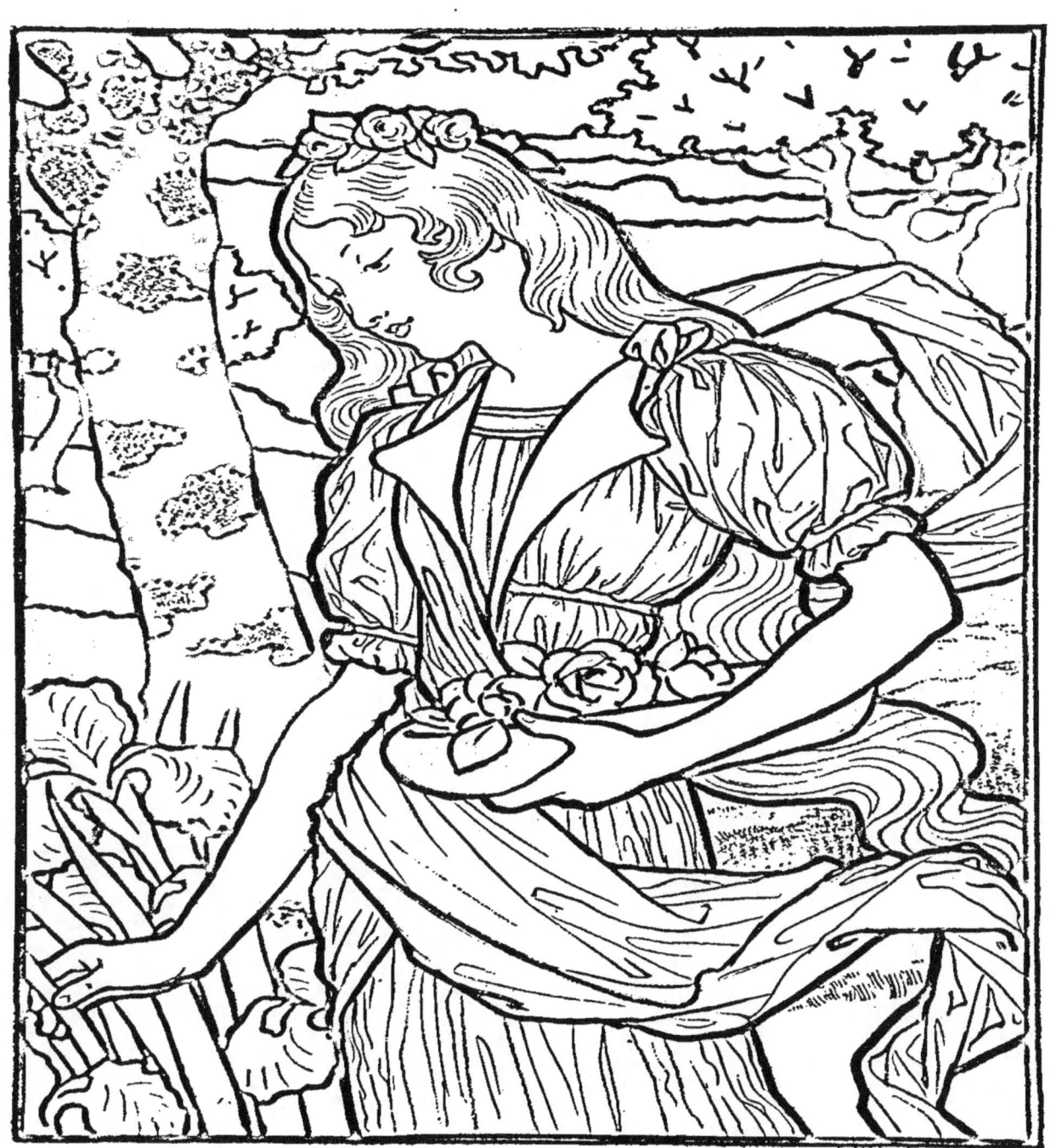